Love is a spark
Lost in the dark
Too soon.

Ogden Nash/Kurt Weill

I like you best
when night is a pleasure you can give.

Janis Ian

Give me new noise, give me new affection
Strange new toys from another world
I need to see more than just 3 dimensions
Stranger than fiction, faster than light.

Tuxedomoon

I sing the body electric.

Walt Whitman

A dimly lit netherworld of lovers
who fell in love
and kept on falling.

Or, of others too proud
to be broken by the catcalls,
the crucifixions.

Lili Lakich

NEON LOVERS GLOW IN THE DARK

LILI LAKICH

MONA
MUSEUM OF NEON ART
Los Angeles, California

➜P
Distributed by Gibbs M. Smith, Inc.
Peregrine Smith Books

Dedicated to my father,
Lt. Col. Ognjan Ivan Lakich, Ret., with love.

ACKNOWLEDGMENTS

I wish to thank Jeff Atherton for his tireless energy and skill in photographing the majority of the work for this book, Danny Justman and Rae Grieco of Typesetting, Ink for their endless efforts on behalf of the typography, and Julie Logan, Jane Handel and Mary Carter for revising the text. Special thanks and much love to Gayle Rendleman and Richard Jenkins for their constant support over a period of many years. And to Mrs. Irby, who was always there when I needed someone to be there.

First Published 1986.

Published on the occasion of the exhibition
Neon Lovers Glow in the Dark: LILI LAKICH
A Retrospective (1965-1985)
at the Museum of Neon Art in Los Angeles
November 6, 1985 - April 26, 1986.

Library of Congress Cataloging-in-Publication Data

Lakich, Lili, 1944-
  Neon lovers glow in the dark.

  1. Lakich, Lili, 1944-   —Exhibitions.   2. Neon sculpture—United States—Exhibitions.   I.
Museum of Neon Art (Los Angeles, Calif.)   II. Title.
NB237.L265A4 1986   730'.92'4   85-18854
ISBN 0-87905-419-0 (Gibbs M. Smith, Inc.)
Distributed by Gibbs M. Smith, Inc.
Peregrine Smith Books, P.O. Box 667, Layton, Utah 84041

Frontispiece:
THE FAVORITE ARTIST:
PORTRAIT OF LILI LAKICH
by Richard Jenkins, 1985
60 x 40" (152 x 102 cm)

TABLE OF CONTENTS

What would Milwaukee be without Schlitz? This early porcelain neon sign was used to board up a window on a shack in New Mexico.

Coney Island tea room, circa 1963.

The desert breeds many curiosities like this one outside of Death Valley.

Neon is the medium of city lights and highway truck-stops, of animated champagne glasses and flickering no-vacancy signs. The image of the neon sign is so familiar, so persistent in the mind's eye, that it becomes an icon of the American city and the American road.

Jonathan Kirsch
NEW WEST, 1978

When my father came home from the Korean War, the first thing he did was buy a brand new, light-blue Chrysler. It was 1953. I was nine years old. In it we travelled all over the United States, visiting relatives and old friends from California to Florida. By day we read all the clever Burma Shave signs and stopped at every souvenir shop or roadside attraction that was made to look like a wigwam, teapot, or giant hamburger. But it was driving at night that I loved best. It was then that the darkness would come alive with brightly colored images of cowboys twirling lassoes atop rearing palominos, sinuous Indians shooting bows and arrows, or huge trucks in the sky with their wheels of light spinning. These were the neon signs attempting to lure motorists to stop at a particular motel or truck-stop diner. It was always the neon signs that I remembered.

In 1956, having moved to Germany courtesy of the U.S. Army, we continued our habitual driving trips; but now we saw a few countries at a time, rather than a few states. Instead of roadside attractions, there were great castles, cathedrals and wonderful art museums.

One of the differences between America and Europe is the tremendous pride that Europeans have in their history. If a significant building is falling down, they just leave it there and call it a ruin—very different from our tendency to tear things down and replace them with the latest architectural trend. It is this regrettable flaw in the American character that has led to the demise of our own home-grown monuments—the carousels, amusement parks, movie palaces, and imaginative, elaborate neon signs.

This book is a record of my own personal journey. What was first glimpsed out the window of our moving car, that is, neon's beckoning flash, evolved into a lifelong passion. As I developed into an artist, it was only logical (and certainly seems so in retrospect) that I would choose neon as my medium, and that it would choose me.

I have always been intrigued by what people put out as the single identifying statement or image of their existence, their place on this earth, whether in the form of a sign, storefront, gravestone, or even tattoo. How they sum up their lives is fascinating, and how they create visual communication forever interests me.

INTRODUCTION

Las Vegas casino.

I'd like to have met this man. Los Angeles, 1975.

A bar in Española, New Mexico.

Store in Albuquerque, New Mexico.

Chinese cafe in Salt Lake City, Utah.

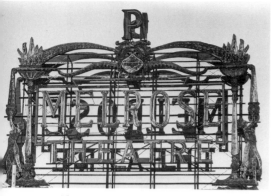

The Melrose Theatre before it was dismantled.

Gayle Rendleman gets ready to lower the lady from the Melrose Theater over the side of the building in this 1974 sign saving expedition.

Grinning up at Gayle and Richard Jenkins after guiding the lady to the ground.

Look alike fast-food franchises can't match the thrill of eating at a unique, oddball cafe like this one in Inglewood, California.

The signs hold a special place in my heart. I grew up looking at them, loving them and examining them for detail. And I've always given them the time they deserve—if there's ever been a sign anywhere I've ever been, I've read it.

Benson, Arizona, used to be a truck-stop for the cross-country highway before Interestate 10 was built and bypassed the town. A neon paradise with spectacular pictorial signs, there was a neon truck the size of a semi in the sky for Marie's Truck Stop, a huge bull for Hank's Coffee Shop, a beautiful gold horse's head inside a horseshoe for the Horseshoe Cafe and even more dazzling beauties. Since the town was bypassed, the businesses have collapsed, for the most part, and so have the neon signs. Notwithstanding all the tradition, all the songs written about it, and all the people who got their kicks on it, Route 66 was recently closed.

Urban centers have become dark, dismal and fearful because the neon which brought brightness, color, liveliness and light into the streets has been removed. Concrete and glass structures just don't have the kind of life that store fronts with neon illumination have. You can go to Las Vegas at 4 a.m., for example, and feel energized, alive, lively—as if life is unending. Here is one of the ugliest places on the face of the earth in the daytime, but at night it is unbelievably beautiful.

Over the years I have been involved in saving and restoring a number of signs that were earmarked for the wrecker's ball. One of the most beautiful is the lady from the Melrose Theatre. Dating back to the twenties, this Paramount theatre had one of the very first electrical rooftop signs. The lady was part of a large "spectacular" designed in the Babylonian style with animating light bulbs. Simulating water originating from both sides of a large face, a ribbon of light flowed to douse flames rising out of a column and fell into urns being held aloft by two women with stars at the ends of their dresses. Neon was used to light the letters.

I find it somewhat boring to travel in America now. Every place you go there's a McDonald's and a Denny's and a Kentucky Fried Chicken and a Motel 6. The unique, one-of-a-kind businesses are disappearing under the thumb of corporate giants. The American dream has given way to the American franchise.

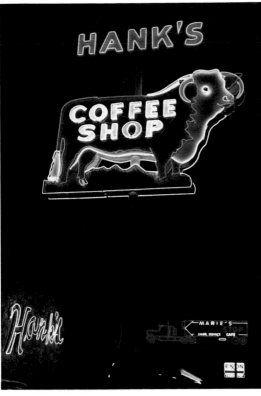

Las Vegas motel.

Hank's Cafe in Benson, Arizona.

Au Diable des Lombards, Paris.

Virgin of Guadalupe, Mexico City.

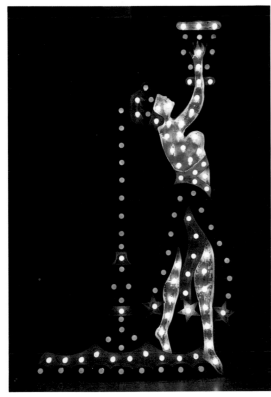

The Melrose Theatre Lady, circa 1920, now in the permanent collection of the Museum of Neon Art. Saved from destruction by Richard Jenkins, Gayle Rendleman, and myself in 1974.

SELF-PORTRAIT WITH NEON
1969
Helium in glass tubing, photo,
plexiglas, aluminum.
18 x 14¼ x 6½ " (46 x 34 x 17 cm)
Collection: Gayle Rendleman,
Los Angeles.

After electricity, I lost interest in nature.
Too backward.

Mayakovsky

SELF-PORTRAIT WITH TEARS
1966
Plexiglas, light bulbs, glass, collage,
paint, wood, motor.
Approx. 48 x 36 x 4"
(122 x 91 x 10 cm)
(Destroyed in a fire, 1980)

Bored by traditional painting, sculpture and graphic arts techniques at Pratt Institute, I left to study filmmaking at The London School of Film Technique. While exciting, filmmaking was too much of a group activity and too much of a compromise. When I came back to Pratt in 1965, I tried to figure out what it was that interested me.

I had always loved pop songs—the melodies, the lyrics, and most importantly, the voices. When Julie London, in her sultry voice sang:

> *Now you say you're lonely*
> *You cried the whole night through.*
> *Well, you can cry me a river.*
> *Cry me a river.*
> *I've cried a river over you.*

I wanted to immortalize that feeling. It bothered me that singers could capture the hearts of the world with blatant sentiments like that while artists, suffering the effects of abstract expressionism and minimalism, were supposed to express themselves in abstraction. Well, I, too, was lonely, and I, too, have cried a river over you, godammit, and wanted to express that in *MY* art.

I thought of using light bulbs but didn't know the first thing about hooking up anything electrically, so when my father came to visit me at Pratt, I enlisted his help in realizing the idea. We went to Canal Street to look for electrical parts. I made a portrait of myself out of plexiglas, and under my eye, drilled holes for tiny light bulbs. We connected them to a motor, and when plugged in, they blinked down my face like tears.

This was my first electrical work of art, and for the first time in my life, I felt that I had really and absolutely expressed myself.

I think that art is a way of packaging emotion and exorcising it. Once I had made a portrait of myself crying, I could stop crying. The sculpture cried for me. If you can express mangled feelings in a work of art, you can overpower them. They then exist as a set of lines, colors and forms. They're no longer an amorphous nausea eating away at your gut. They're incorporated into an object. You can see it. And if you can make the thing beautiful, you can somehow feel that it has sanctity . . . that it is an icon capable of arousing an emotional response in other people as well.

P L A T E S   A N D   T E X T

THEY CALL ME NIGGER,
THEY CALL ME CHOCOLATE
1970
Argon with mercury in glass
tubing, plexiglas, animator.
52 x 44 x 6″ (132 x 112 x 15 cm)

Lloyd Ziff at Pratt Institute in 1967. Years later, while commiserating over the failure of our latest relationships, he made his legendary statement, ''We are more interesting than any of our lovers have been.'' He is now an art director with Condé Nast Publications.

Bonnie considered herself to be a ''white witch,'' one who casts only good spells.

Lloyd Ziff (February 26, 1967): "I read something great in *Ship of Fools* that I meant to tell you. Let me see if I can remember it. This probably isn't exact, but it's almost right." And he wrote down:

Love me!
Even if I am not worthy of Love
Even if you are not capable of Love
Even if there is no such thing as Love.
Love me!

I met Bonnie at Lloyd's apartment in Brooklyn. She was a magnificent Black woman, a lioness, with one of the most beautiful voices I had ever heard. At 25, she had a 3-year old half-black, half-Indian son, and told us that she'd had the child so that she could get on welfare. She drew or painted her fantasies and was very prolific. I went to her apartment on the Lower East Side and was amazed to see several paintings of someone who looked exactly like me. It was as if I were a fantasy come to life.

Bonnie considered herself to be a witch and occasionally performed a spell with bubbling, smoking, green water. Her fears of the powers of witchcraft were enormous. If one did not follow all the procedures for casting a spell precisely (she had a thick book with all the steps of many different spells carefully laid out), then the spell would backfire. It was a mystery to me.

Once, in a conversation, she said, ''They call me nigger, they call me chocolate.''

Whether coincidence or fate, it just so happened that I had a neon of the word ''Chocolate.'' It was the first scrap neon tube that had been given to me by the sign company in Queens, New York where I first went to find out how to go about working with the medium. They were very sweet. They also gave me a small white heart and a transformer and drew me a diagram of how to wire it all together.

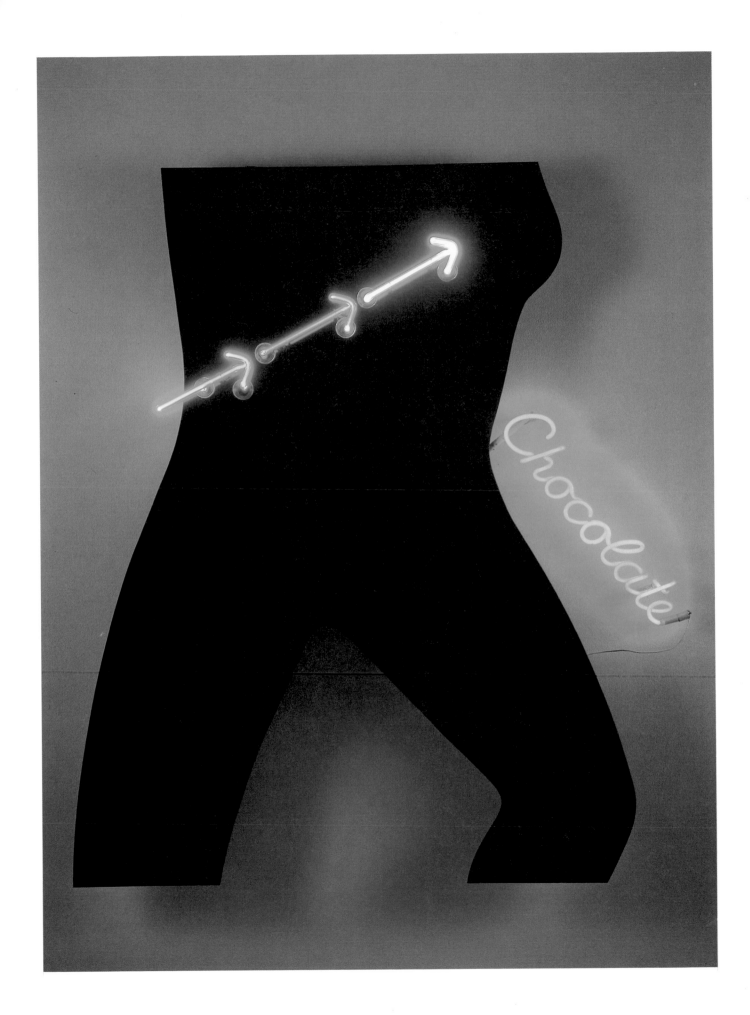

LOVE IN VAIN (Drawing), 1969. Colored pencil, pen, photo. 11¼ x 10″ (29 x 25 cm).

8/19/72

DRAW ME NEARER, 1972. Colored pencil, pen, photo. 12 ½ x 9″ (32 x 23 cm). Collection: Anni Siegel Jackson, Los Angeles.

DON'T JUMP UP AND DOWN
ON MY TOES, YOU LOVED
ME ONCE, YOU KNOW
1972
Argon with mercury, neon and
helium in glass tubing, photo,
painted metal, animator.
96 x 72 x 12″ (244 x 183 x 30 cm)

At work in 1971.

Forms drawn onto the metal case changed
somewhat during the fabrication process.

Fastening the first neon tube to the metal case.

D*on't Jump Up and Down On My Toes, You Loved Me Once, You Know* came from a song lyric by Melanie in the sixties. It was such an off-the-wall, gut-level sentiment that it stuck with me for years. In 1971 I set about to express that feeling in a neon sculpture.

I found the face in a *LIFE* magazine article on heroin addiction and had used it in a number of drawings during the late 60's and early 70's. Since love, too, is a drug, the connection was perfect. I had a large blow-up made of the photo, mounted it on masonite, covered it with plexi and bolted it to an 8-foot metal case that I had built. I took over the living room to do the work. Since I could only afford a few pieces of neon at a time, I lit them as I got them, and the sculpture evolved slowly.

I wanted the sculpture to animate but was wary of how repetitious and boring animating neon could be. The only sign with moving neon that was not boring to me was on a bar in Hollywood called The Speak 39. It had some stars and zoom shapes which animated so erratically that I could never figure out what it was going to do next. I spent a long time on many different occasions studying that animation sequence. When the movement on *Don't Jump. . .* was complete, I was pleased that it was not predictable but rather hypnotic.

Nate Prusan who bent all the tubing came to see the finished product. He stared at it for about an hour and finally said, "This is better than watching T.V."

VACANCY/NO VACANCY
1973
Argon with mercury and neon in
glass tubing, stainless steel,
aluminum, animator.
31 x 27 x 8″ (79 x 69 x 20 cm)
Collection: Marion Rothman,
Studio City, California.

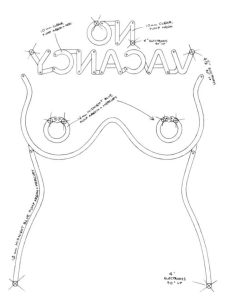

Little did I realize when I brought the pattern for
No Vacancy to a neon shop that I would be chas-
tised and lectured about God and sin and eternal
life. It was a family business, and they were all
Jehovah's Witnesses. Noticing the naked Playboy
pin-ups hanging on the walls, I pointed them out
to the man who went right on preaching about
Satan and damnation. I then said, "But you do all
the neon for The Pink Pussycat Theatres (a chain
of porno movie theatres)." It didn't phase him; he
was hell-bent on saving my soul. I had to take my
pattern elsewhere. After that I drew my patterns
so the lines that made up an image were scram-
bled and you couldn't tell what it was until the
neon was all assembled.

It's not the spotlight.
It's not the candlelight.
It's not the moonlight
Shining down on me.
It's not the sunlight.
Not even the neon light.
But you see it shining in my eyes.
And you know what that means.

Barry Goldberg/Gerry Goffin

There is an emotional and a spiritual quality to light that remains elusive despite sporadic attempts to define the effects of certain kinds of light or colors of light. Frequently associated with banal images of crass commercialism, neon has always been linked with motels, shops of all kinds, theatres, and dens of iniquity.

The truth is that neon exudes a quality of warmth, gaiety, and friend-liness that is not possible with fluorescent or incandescent light. The colors, the sinewy lines, the ability of the medium to depict imagery that glows from itself is perhaps an updated version of religious iconography that emanated light. Jesus glowed; the Virgin of Guadalupe glowed. For me there was always a link between those glowing religious symbols and images in neon which also emit light.

I chose the medium of neon because no one had considered it a medium worthy of fine art. It was a medium for advertising, not art. (And advertising sleazy bars, shoe repair shops and cheap motels at that.) I felt there was some sort of connection between the stigma of neon and the equal contempt with which emotions are regarded in our culture. We are given support for denying our emotions, for not being "hung up," for not wallowing in depression or pain, for not expressing an opinion for fear of hurting someone. I believe in emotion. I believe in wallowing in it.

It was these connections that led me to create *Vacancy/No Vacancy*, a contemporary madonna who put forward her availability or lack of it in no uncertain terms. A flick of the switch will change her from an open and willing seeker of intimacy to a woman who needs nothing from anyone. It's a woman's prerogative to change her mind, after all. Oddly enough, it has become a favorite of feminist-oriented exhibitions in both the United States and in Europe.

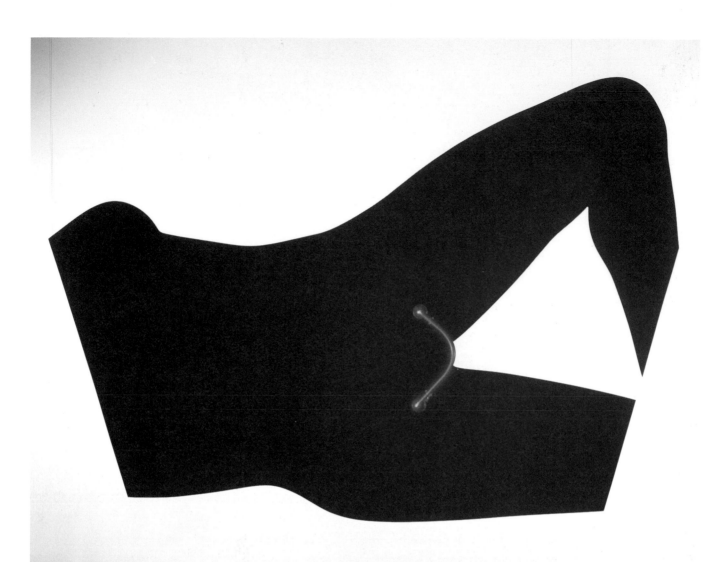

THE RED HOT MAMA
1973
Lacquered candy apple paint on
masonite with neon tube.
67 x 48 x 5″ (170 x 122 x 13 cm)
Collection: Murray Pepper,
Beverly Hills, California.

HUNG UP ON YOU
1973
Helium in glass tubing, stainless
steel, plexiglas.
35 x 49 x 8″ (89 x 124 x 20 cm)
Collection: Museum of Neon Art,
gift of Tony Seiniger, Los Angeles.

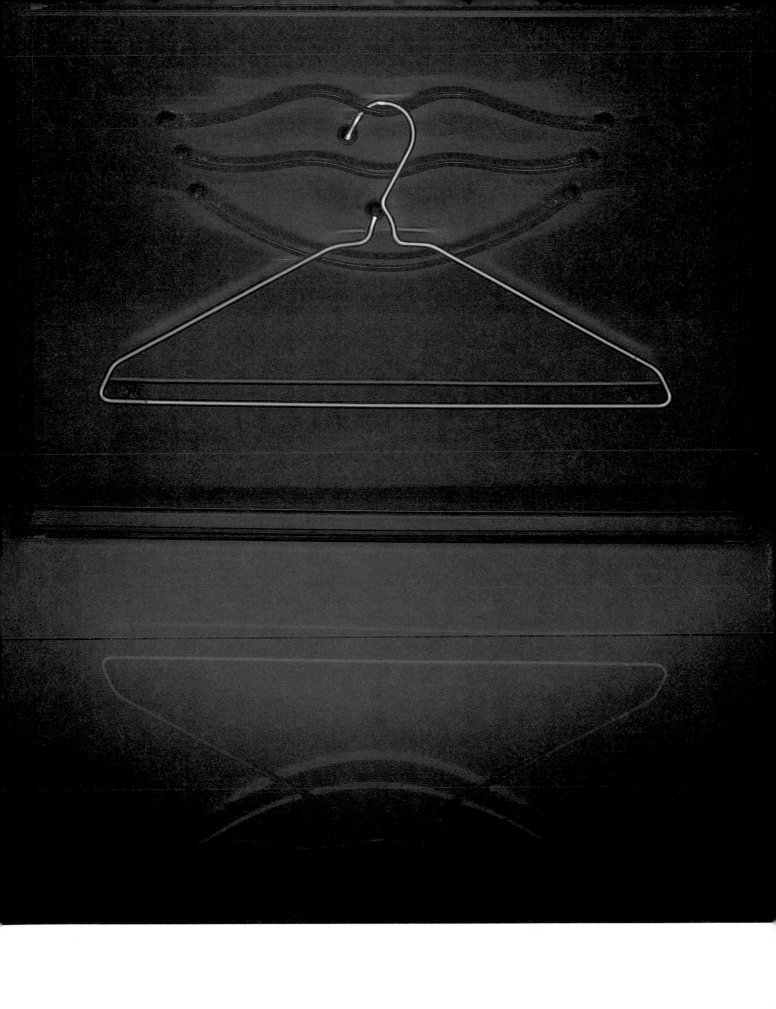

SCAR
1974
Argon with mercury and helium in
glass tubing, painted metal.
108 x 84 x 12″ (274 x 213 x 30 cm)

This U.S. Army insignia was the reference for the panther head.

Tattoo parlors at "The Pike" in Long Beach provided inspiration for *Scar, Blessed Oblivion, Draw Me Nearer, Death Before Dishonor, Val's Cafe* and other work of this period.

Scar was first exhibited at Womanspace in The Woman's Building in 1974.

By 1974 I had already filled up the house with my neon sculpture, so I next moved to the garage in order to build *Scar*. It was an old garage that leaked, and I could only stand back about five feet from the metal case to which the neon tubes were attached. But I was determined to build it as large as possible under the circumstances.

I wanted *Scar* to express the feeling of the Dylan Thomas poem, "Do not go gentle into that good night, Rage, rage against the dying of the light." The central image of the snarling panther was chosen from an embroidered army patch. Having been raised in the military, I was familiar with the symbols of all the armies, divisions, battalions, etc. This one was my favorite. I also spent a lot of time looking at tattoos, particularly at "The Pike" in Long Beach. The blood drops were borrowed from Edvard Munch.

When I finished *Scar* and lit it up for the first time in that scroungy garage, it was magical. It was voodoo, hocus pocus, heebie jeebie and helter skelter. And it raged, raged against the dying of the light.

The working drawing for the sculpture.

BLESSED OBLIVION
1975
Argon with mercury and neon in
glass tubing, painted metal, plastic
flowers.
126 x 108 x 12″ (320 x 274 x 30 cm)

Gayle Rendleman's wit and intelligence without
"wanting to do anything with it" provided the
original inspiration for *Blessed Oblivion*. She is
immortalized as the panther.

Drilling holes into the metal case through the
paper pattern.

In 1975 I decided that I wanted to create a tombstone for the living dead. I was interested in building a monument to those people who are not concerned with leaving their mark on the world or in striving for any sort of immortality. I wondered what demons, if any, they struggled with knowing that they had not done anything significant with their lives.

It took me a year of drawing different images into the basic tombstone shape before I arrived at the tattoo image of the embattled panther and python. The death angel above was taken from early New England gravestone markings. In order to get some reference for the forms, I searched out tattoo parlors in Los Angeles and Long Beach. At the time, it was almost impossible to photograph any of the flash (i.e. tattoo design) cards. To do so was to jeopardize one's life. I was chased out of a few tattoo parlors for being too curious. Finally, I was able to photograph the design I needed as reference for the panther and python with a telephoto lens from across the street. The title came from a tattoo I saw on a young actor who played in a "D" movie that used some of my sculptures as a set. On his forearm he had tattooed:

BLESSED

BLESSED

OBLIVION

I built the major portion of the piece but couldn't come up with anything for the left side. It stayed unfinished for months while I drew different images into that section. One day some friends came to my studio for dinner, and they brought me some cymbidiums from their garden. I looked at the flowers and taped them to the sculpture, and it worked. I drew the vase and table to support them and *Blessed Oblivion* was finished at long last.

Many things have been said about the sculpture, but the greatest comment was made by Mr. Quilez, the father of a friend of mine. An Argentine of Basque origin, he looked at the work for several minutes, then turned to me and said, "You are a giant."

24

Blessed Oblivion

GOODBYE
1973
Argon with helium in glass tubing,
stainless steel, wood.
44 x 40 x 8″ (112 x 102 x 20 cm)
Collection: Gayle Rendleman,
Los Angeles.

In the company of plaster figures at Old Trapper's
Lodge in Sun Valley, California, 1983.

The Big Horn Restaurant in Amado, Arizona, was
built in 1970 and epitomizes the Western aesthetic.

When I left New York City in 1968 for the West Coast, I worried that my aesthetic, which was just forming out of the bright lights, big city atmosphere of the East, might be perverted into something that resembled Cowboy art. After all, California was the home of Hollywood, steeped in the tradition of westerns upon which I had been raised— Roy Rogers, Hopalong Cassidy, or my favorite, Zorro.

After travelling around the world during 30 years of military service, my parents retired outside of Fort Huachuca, Arizona. I hated the desert at first. Barren, dusty, flat landscape with scraggly vegetation of cactus and mesquite trees couldn't compare to the lush green rolling hills of Pennsylvania and Maryland. My visits, having begun as painful excursions into the mindset of the Old West, became increasingly more enjoyable as I grew to love the quiet yet spectacular beauty of the desert. Driving through Monument Valley and Death Valley was one of the most profoundly moving of all my experiences, and when I saw the dinosaur under construction along Interstate 10 coming into California, I knew I was in the right place.

I love seeing the continuing tradition of Indian art—the sandpaintings, the Kachinas, the masks. *Spirit* is my version of an Indian rain god.

The truck-stop dinosaur in Cabazon, California
was under construction in 1968.

One day while bored at my job, I made some ink
blots. This one became the inspiration for the
image of *Death Before Dishonor* on the next
page.

26

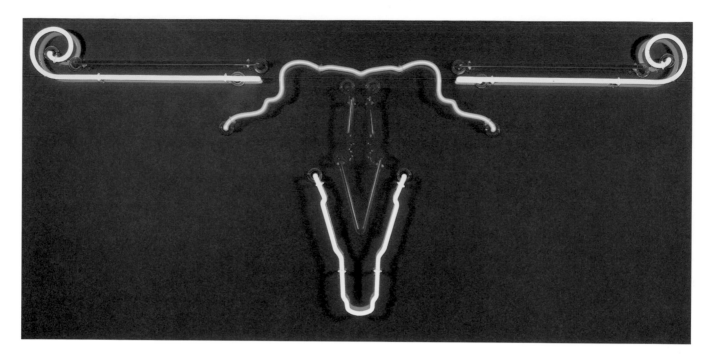

DEATH BEFORE DISHONOR
1972
Argon with mercury and neon in
glass tubing, lacquered metal,
aluminum.
76 x 36 x 12″ (193 x 91 x 30 cm)

Installation view at the Museum of Neon Art during my retrospective
exhibition, *Neon Lovers Glow in the Dark,* 1985-86.

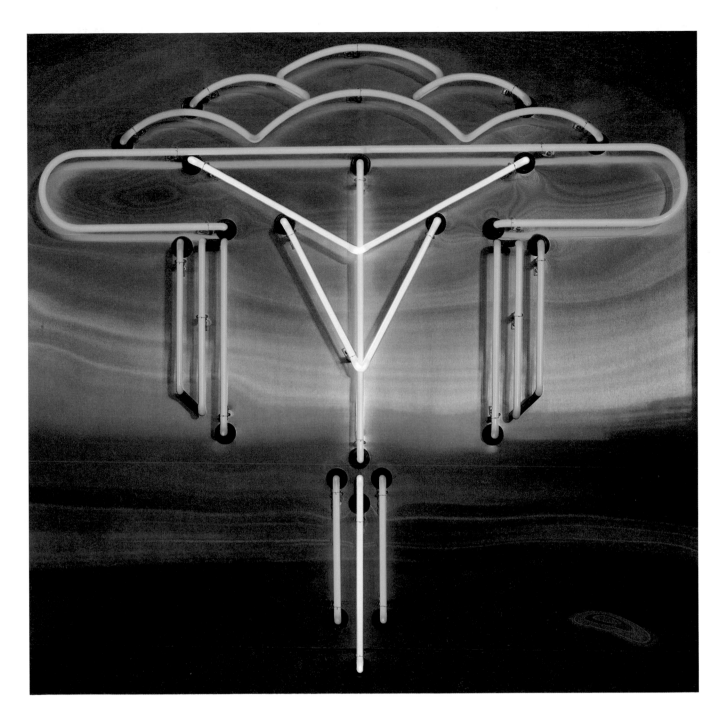

SPIRIT
1975
Argon in glass tubing, stainless
steel, wood.
49 x 48½ x 8″ (124 x 123 x 20 cm)

DON'T
1975
Argon with mercury and helium in
glass tubing, film positive.
60 x 48″ (152 x 122 cm)
Collection: Tom O'Brien,
Los Angeles.

One of the people I met at *CYCLE NEWS* was
Tom Walsh, a young poet, who functioned as the
advertising manager. He, too, was interested in
the signs people make to express themselves.

A weekly motorcycle newspaper, *CYCLE NEWS,* gave me my first job in Southern California. I started out printing photos for the layouts and ended up as art director. Having experimented ad nauseum with endless variations of the motorcycle theme, I was intrigued by this photograph hanging in the bathroom of a friend. I don't know where it came from. It had an air of contempt that was missing from all the photos I was accustomed to seeing at the newspaper.

I blew up the photo onto film, added a few neon tubes, a pinch of glitter and presto! An invincible Amazon.

WISH YOU WERE HERE
1976
Argon, helium and krypton in glass
tubing, porcelain on steel.
135 x 108 x 12″ (343 x 274 x 30 cm)

Cat's Paw shoe repair box.

I always thought I had the same eyes as this cat.

One of the stupidest things I learned in art school was that black is not a color. The teachers kept insisting that black was the absence of color. The Impressionists never used black, and they were supposed to be the definitive experts on color and light. Well, black just so happens to be my favorite color; the only thing that black may be the absence of is a lover.

Wish You Were Here is built on a steel case with porcelain enamel. Porcelain enamel is melted down glass that is sprayed onto the surface of a rigid metal and then baked. It is the most durable kind of coloring possible. Early neon signs were made with porcelain on steel backgrounds, and the colors look just as vibrant today as they did 50 years ago. In attempting to choose the color for the zig zag case, I spent three days looking through over 2000 color chips. I ended up choosing black.

When I first came to Southern California, I hated palm trees. They represented a leisure time attitude of lolling about on the beach, cultivating one's skin cancer. It took four years in order for me just to tolerate them. Since it's become clear to me that there is no place else I'd rather be, now I quite like the palms.

I appropriated the Cat's Paw emblem because it's one of my favorite images. Comic book symbols have always fascinated me for their ingenious ambiguity.

HONKY TONK ANGEL
(Portrait of Pam Bennett)
1977
Argon with mercury, helium and
krypton in glass tubing, porcelain
on steel.
96 x 72 x 12″ (244 x 183 x 30 cm)

Pam Bennett in Mexico City, 1976.

There was neon around every painting and statue
throughout this church in Mexico City. Notice the
transformer on the wall in the upper left hand
corner.

Sometimes an exchange of words can get under my skin to the extent that an image will emerge unconsciously. One day I was just doodling. I put down a few lines and realized that those few lines looked exactly like my friend Pam. And the snake on a stick next to her, was the precise symbol for her ability to manipulate phrases and people.

I had met Pam Bennett when I came back to work for Seiniger Advertising after having worked for another company for a while. We were drawn to one another largely because of an interesting verbal repartee. In 1976 we traveled to Mexico City together, and it was there that I discovered the neon church. A poor people's church, the neon served as a substitute for stained glass and gold leaf. The neon was everywhere—as crowns on the paintings of the Virgin, as border tubing around statues of Jesus, and as words proclaiming "Providencia" and "Ave Maria." I was ecstatic, and I went back to Mexico City on another occasion in order to experience its unique, spectacular ambiance. I was fascinated; it confirmed all of my beliefs in the spiritual qualities of neon light.

It was after returning to our hotel room that this exchange took place.

Pam: *And did you pray for me too?*
Lili: *Yes.*
Pam: *What did you pray for?*
Lili: *That I wouldn't have to endure any more of your gray lies.*
Pam: *What color would you like them to be? I can make them any color you like.*

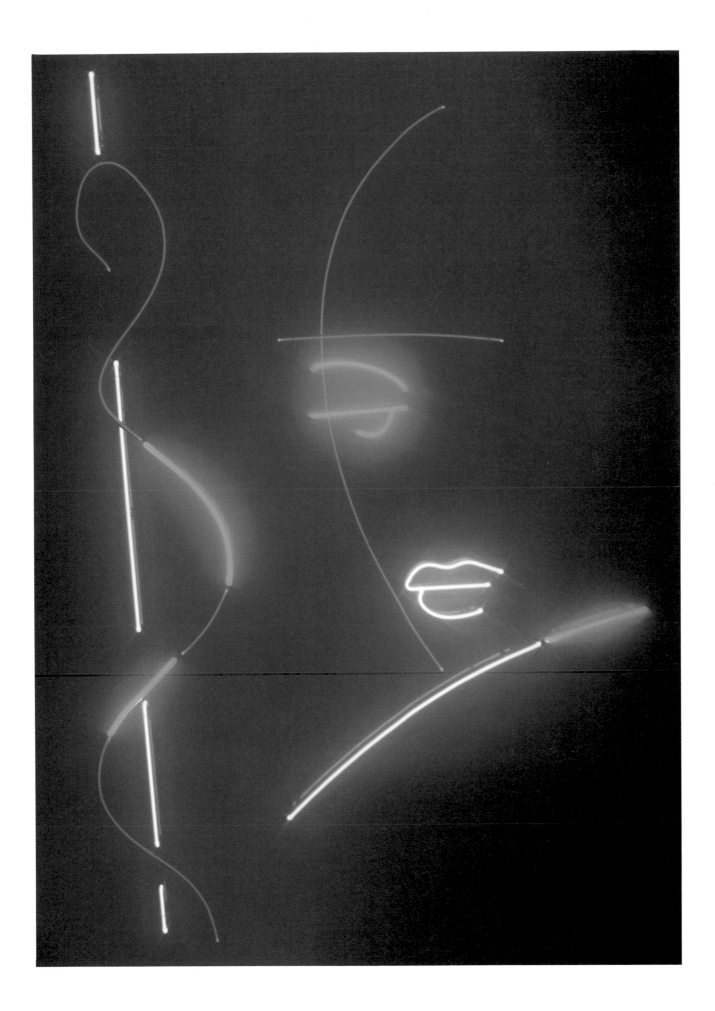

SELF-PORTRAIT WITH SNEER
1977
Helium and krypton in glass
tubing, porcelain on steel.
96 x 72 x 12" (244 x 183 x 30 cm)

She's got everything she needs
She's an artist she don't look back
She can take the dark out of the nighttime
And paint the daytime black.

Bob Dylan

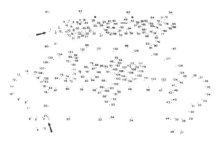

This connect-a-dot puzzle by Gracie Mansion was created for the Sofa/Painting Show at Gracie Mansion Gallery, New York in 1983.

One of my favorite artists is Alexej Jawlensky. This is *Abstract Head Nr. 20,* painted in 1921.

I wanted to be the one to take the dark out of the nighttime. One of my favorite activities as a kid was drawing the lines that connected numbered dots to reveal a picture in puzzle books. Fascinating also were the constellations formed when lines joined certain stars together.

Drawing with neon tubes is similar as each tube has an electrode on either end that fits into a glass receptacle called a housing. The housings are screwed into holes that are drilled into the background. The tubes connect the holes, and when wires are connected from the housings to the transformers, the tubes light up.

The amount of rejection that any artist suffers from gallery dealers, museum curators, competition jurors, publishers, critics, etc. is staggering. (Recently I talked with a writer whose marvelous book was rejected 70 times before being published.) To this day (in 1985), none of my work has ever been accepted by any juried art competition, and I have sent slides to quite a lot of them.

Once when I sent my slides for consideration to the Whitney Museum's biennial exhibition, I received a letter back describing my work as "wonderfully ferocious" but not acceptable for their purposes. In a review for one of my solo exhibitions, a critic wrote, "Lili Lakich's neon sculptures are like tongue sandwiches. Either you like them, or you don't. I do." Having my work compared to a tongue sandwich, however much she likes them, is an abuse I would rather avoid.

The self-portrait that emerged at this time just naturally had a sneer. And sometimes I do believe that spitefulness is next to godliness.

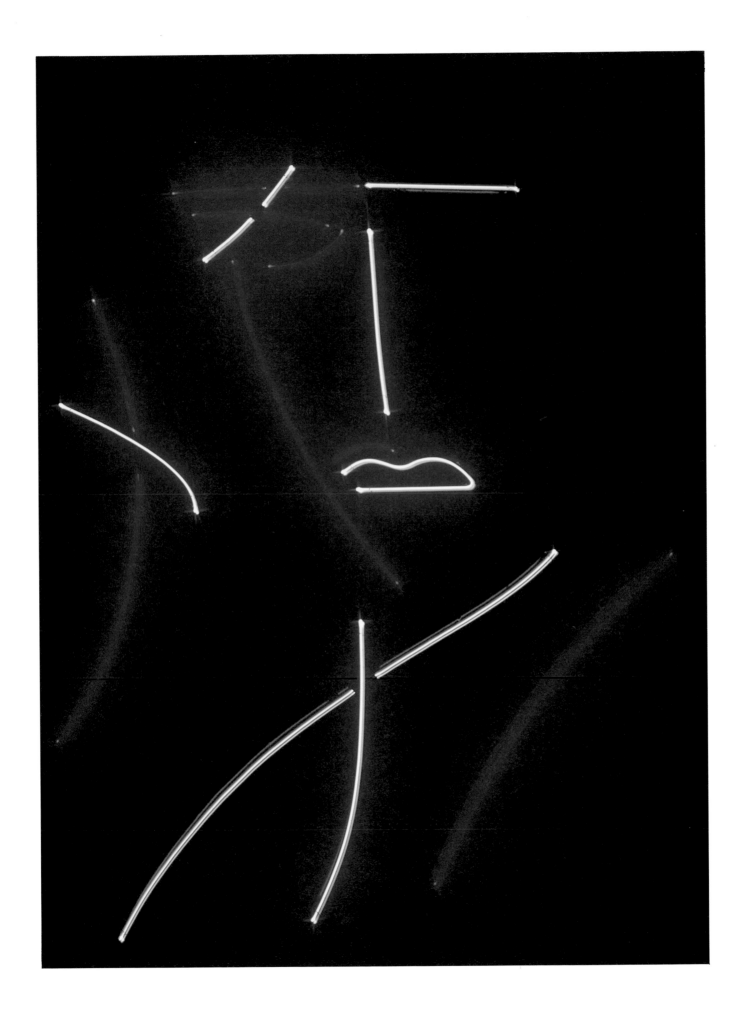

OASIS: PORTRAIT OF DJUNA
BARNES
1977
Argon with mercury in glass tubing
on painted metal.
96 x 72 x 11" (244 x 183 x 28 cm)

This photo of Djuna Barnes, from the New
Directions edition of *Nightwood,* was taken in
Paris in 1921. It provided the original inspiration
for the sculpture.

One of the most beautiful packages is this one
designed by M. Ponty. I looked at it for both the
color and the smoke.

Frank Sinatra once said, "I'm for anything that can help you make it through the night." For me, that "anything" has been *Nightwood* by Djuna Barnes. First published in 1936, it is a story of obsessive love and love's relation to the night. Written in a beautiful prose style, it is the best book I have ever read. *Oasis: Portrait of Djuna Barnes* was inspired by the photo of Barnes on the book's back cover, and I have created three versions of the piece in different colors.

I went to Paris in 1978 to do a show at Galerie au Fond de la Cour in the St. Germaine des Prés district where *Nightwood* is set. As I walked daily along the same streets that were written about in the book fifty years ago, it all seemed exactly the same. The book came alive. I was thrilled.

Neon was perfected in Paris in 1910 by Georges Claude whose invention of the non-corroding electrode stabilized the phenomenon of electrifying gas in a glass tube, allowing it to last for decades. For years he held the patent, and anyone who wished to set up a neon manufacturing shop had to buy a franchise from him at an exorbitant sum. Naturally, I thought that Paris would have all the supplies I needed and possibly even things I hadn't dreamed of. To my shock there were only eight colors of tubing available, and they were all pastel. Having never had a pastel thought in my life, I was devastated. After about three weeks of near catatonic stupor, I set about to rework all of my patterns into pastels.

I spent 3½ months in Paris building ten sculptures for exhibition at a very small gallery at the end of a courtyard. In my walks around the area I frequently heard a woman singing in an unusual style that I can only describe as "electric" improvisation, possibly somewhat akin to Portuguese fado singing. She accompanied herself on a ukelele and would position herself in a courtyard-like arrangement of buildings where the acoustics were particularly keen. She always drew a large crowd. I asked her if she would sing at the opening of my show, and she agreed. The show, with its luminous, pastel neon sculptures and her wild, phenomenal, electric voice echoing about the courtyard, fairly levitated with energy and vibrancy. It was as close as I've come to Heaven.

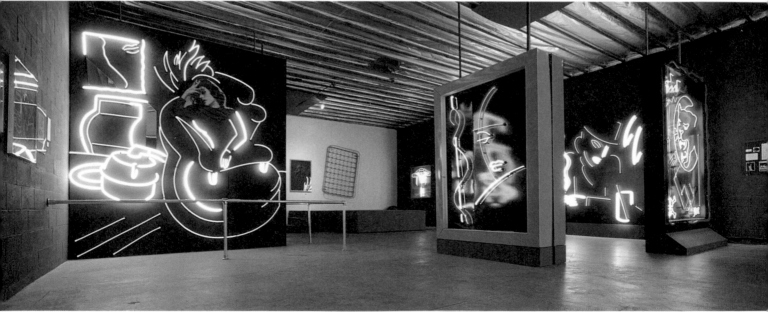

Installation views of my retrospective exhibition, *Neon Lovers Glow in the Dark,* at the Museum of Neon Art, 1985-86.

Opposite page:
SIDEWINDER
(Portrait of Robin Blaiwes)
1977
Helium and krypton in glass
tubing, copper, plexiglas.
50 x 34 x 8″ (127 x 86 20 cm)

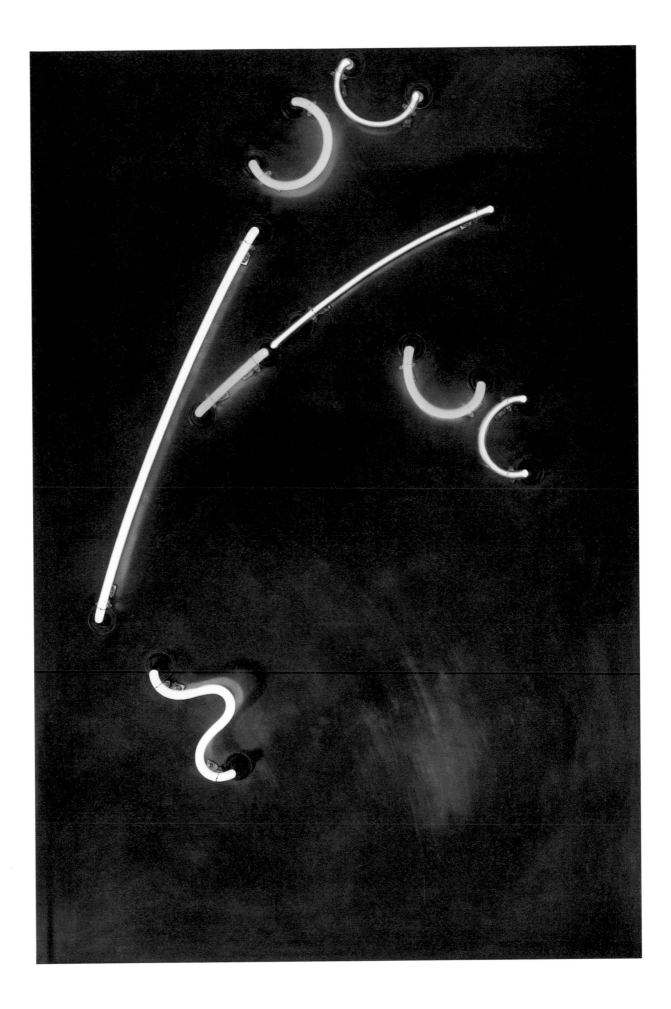

LOVE IN VAIN
1977
Argon with mercury, helium and
krypton in glass tubing, photo,
plexiglas, painted metal.
137 x 122 x 12″ (348 x 311 x 15 cm)

Still, I feel as if
your lips have been
amputated from mine.

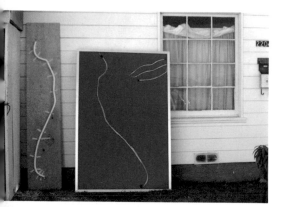

In the upper left hand corner of *Love In Vain* is
an image which in fact was a neon piece I had
built in 1969 titled *Woman*. I worked on it in the
front yard of a very small house in Redondo
Beach. Anni Siegel used to say that I was the only
person she knew who could spend two months
drawing a single line. The form of the woman is
one of the lines I spent two months drawing.

Standing in front of *Love In Vain* at my solo
exhibition sponsored by L.A. Louver Gallery in
1977.

Building *Love In Vain* as a 12-foot monument was perhaps my greatest personal triumph. I did the drawing of it in 1969 and thought it had a lot of feeling and meaning. But people I showed it to didn't know what to say about it. I think they were somewhat embarrassed to see an image so emotionally raw and bizarre at the same time. A woman as an overstuffed chair? What did it mean? What were those things around her head? Why the vacuum cleaner? Was there some deep, dark secret meaning that they just weren't getting? The reactions to the drawing were not very encouraging.

There was something about the drawing that was very powerful for me. The utter immobility brought on by the destruction of a love affair. And your head won't leave you alone thinking about it. Robin Morgan wrote of the excuses for not moving, and Djuna Barnes warned, "... be careful whom you love—for a lover who dies, no matter how forgotten, will take somewhat of you to the grave."

Eight years later this idea still meant a lot to me, and I had the courage to build it into a gargantuan tribute to *Love In Vain*. Initially, half of the tubes were red. The woman looked as if she were burning in hell. It was disastrous; I was very depressed. Each color of tubing was connected to a different transformer, and one day as I was plugging them into the wall the transformer for the red tubes was the last one to be plugged in. In looking at the sculpture with the red tubes off, I was amazed at how beautiful it was as the color combination of flesh colors and shades of white was very unusual. I then took all the red tubes back to the glassbender and had them repumped with krypton gas. They now look grey.

SAVING GRACE
1977
Helium in glass tubing, stainless
steel, plexiglas.
47 x 41¼ x 8″ (119 x 105 x 20 cm)

Detail from an Indian sandpainting.

I've been looking at Saving Grace *for a few weeks now,
or longer.
I couldn't write anything; could hardly look sometimes,
because the bottom of sorrow was there—
an empty column in my own body, squeezed by an internal hand
locked with the set of my jaw—
and I was trying to avoid it.
The expression in the face of your drawing absorbs me
and draws me into the darkness.
The blackness, the brooding, the curl of the lip,
are recessive.
The small spots of color are scar, shock, recoil.
I recognize the point of sorrow which we know, and which
opens to our return.
I stare into the face of all that has not worked out
in my life.*

Arlene Raven
July 17, 1977
excerpted from *CHRYSALIS* No. 5, p. 56.

WOMAN IN TRENCHCOAT
1978
Argon with mercury and helium in
glass tubing, copper, plexiglas.
50¼ x 30¾ x 8″ (127 x 78 x 20 cm)
Collection: Nicholas von Sternberg, Jr.,
Venice, California.

*The sculptures, even the tubes
themselves are jewels salvaged from
the modern world, transformed into
icons of glistening beauty made all
the more startling by their garish
origins.*

Dell Richards
from *NO VACANCY*

On the way to Death Valley in 1977, Dell Richards
posed in front of one of my very favorite desert
cowgirls in Baker, California.

This is another example of a collection of lines looking like somebody after the fact of having been drawn. Dell Richards never wore a trenchcoat, but the piece looked so much like her that she will always be the *Woman In Trenchcoat.*

One day Nicholas von Sternberg, Jr. came to my studio and asked me if I wanted to know how to photograph my work. Neon is extremely difficult to photograph, especially if the neon is not the bright, vibrant street colors but rather the dim, subtle gasses in dark glass. I said yes, of course, but why didn't he photograph them for me himself? He didn't really want to, but then I said, "I'll make something for you. How about this?" I showed him a very rough sketch of *Woman in Trenchcoat.* It was a deal, and I was so pleased that he believed in the sculpture from seeing only a rough sketch.

I didn't know what I was in for. Photographing my neon sculpture was a long, grueling process. I had to rewire each sculpture so that each color was lit separately and photographed at a different exposure time. Nick would calculate each exposure on a slide rule. Some shots had up to nine separate exposures on one piece of film.

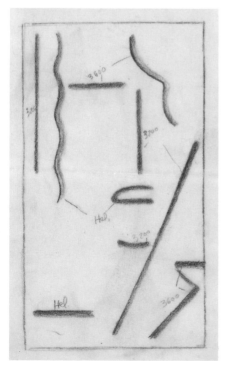

My rough sketches are usually so rough that I am
always amazed at the finished result.

Following right hand page:
THE WARRIOR
(Portrait of Robin Tyler)
1980
Helium and krypton in glass
tubing; copper, plexiglas.
60½ x 37½ x 8″ (154 x 95 x 20 cm)

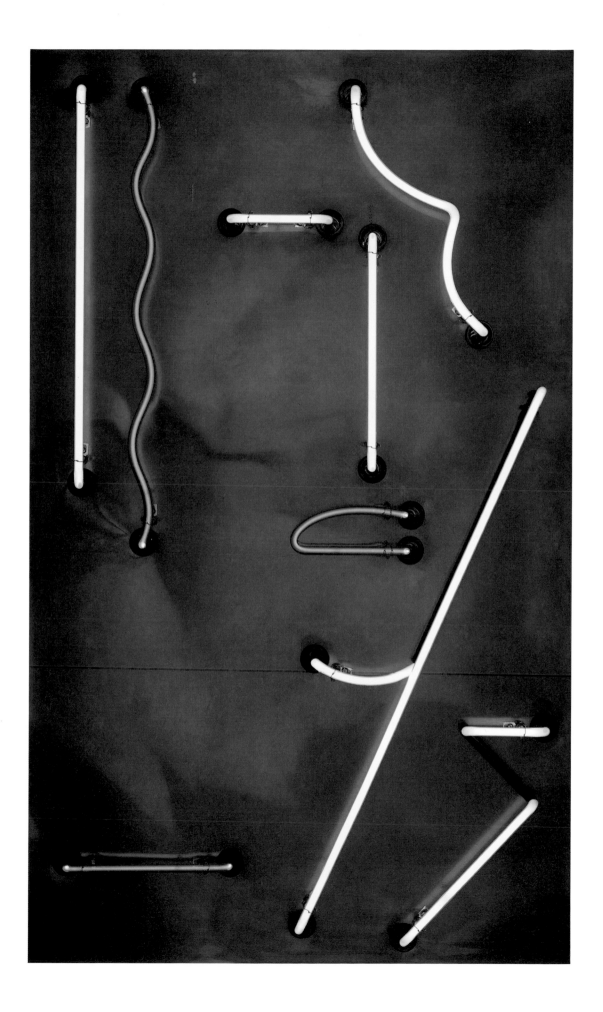

THE WARRIOR, 1979. Colored pencil on matt board. Collection: Fernando Lozano, Los Angeles.

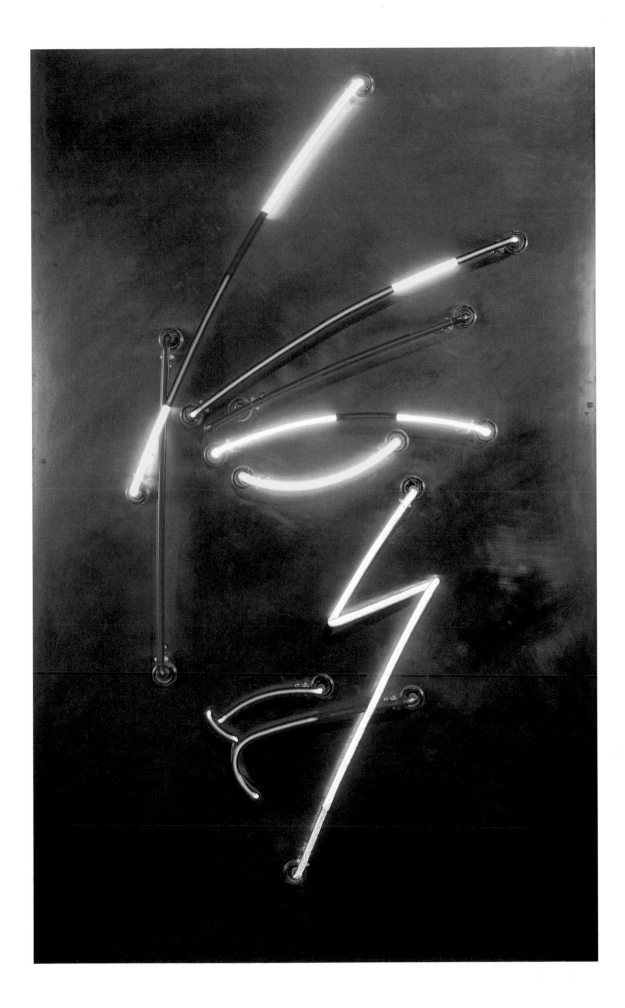

PORTRAIT OF A PUNK
1978
Colored pencil on matt board.
31 x 27½ " (79 x 70 cm)

PORTRAIT OF A PUNK
1980-1982
Argon with mercury and neon in
glass tubing, metal, paint.
65 x 57½ x 8″ (165 x 146 x 20 cm)
Collection: Richard Jenkins,
Los Angeles.

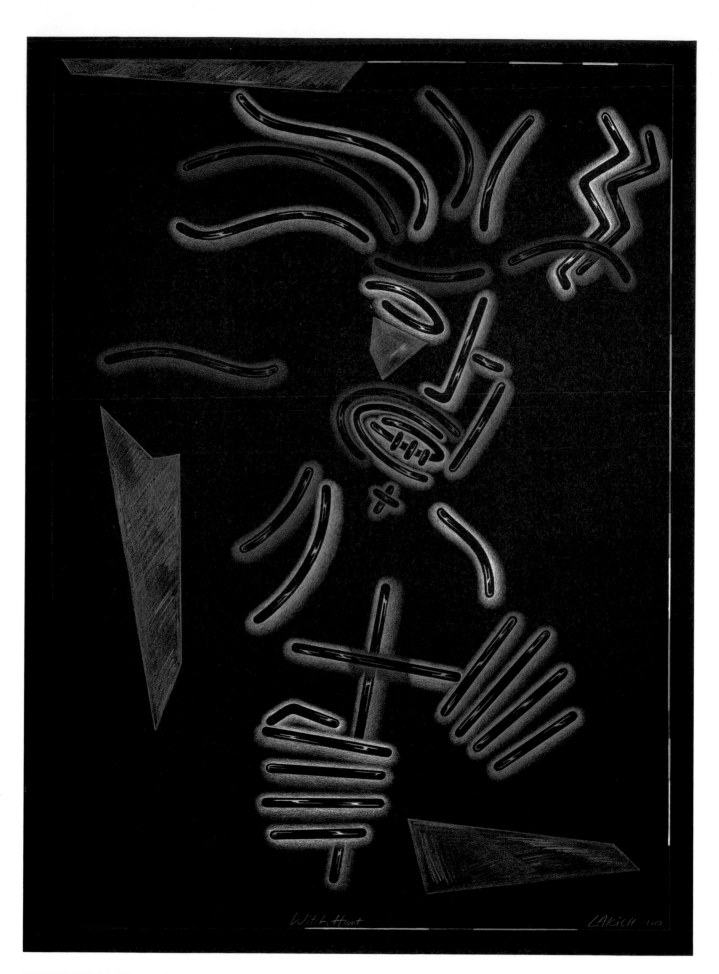

WITCH HUNT, 1980. Colored pencil on matt board. 39 x 30″ (99 x 76 cm).

THE PHOENIX, 1980. Colored pencil on matt board. 31¼ x 22½ (79 x 57 cm).

THE DEERHUNTER
1981
Argon with mercury and helium in
glass tubing, aluminum, paint.
49½ x 42 x 7" (126 x 107 x 18 cm)

Are you working on something new?
Yes.
Anything exciting?
Are you exciting?
Sometimes.
Well, actually . . . I'm working on you.

From a conversation
with Robin Blaiwes

Richard Jenkins with members of "The Mystic Knights of the Oingo Boingo."

Packing *The Deerhunter* to send to The New Museum in New York, 1981.

T*he Deerhunter* came from a combination of influences. I was designing a brochure for the movie of that name and was haunted by the scenes of Russian roulette and the bandannas worn by the players. I had just taken another road trip through Monument Valley and had stopped at dozens of trading posts and souvenir shops to look at Kachina dolls and masks. Also, during that period I had been looking at photographs of Richard Jenkins wearing white make-up and red lips in performances of "The Mystic Knights of the Oingo Boingo" years before. These red and white and black images converged in *The Deerhunter* which has retained the mystical presence of its conception.

This sculpture marks my first use of honeycomb aluminum. It proved to be such a perfect material for my needs that I was sorry that I hadn't discovered it sooner. It is extremely lightweight (I would no longer need four gorillas to move my sculpture), and it is perfectly rigid (neon doesn't like any torque). Although I had cut out a few forms before, most of my work was confined to a rectangular format. Since honeycomb aluminum is fairly easy to cut with a small saber saw, I started breaking up the rectangles. The sculpture was spray-painted, and for the first time I painted parts of the neon tubes black.

ST. VALENTINE
1983
Argon with mercury, helium and
neon in glass tubing; aluminum,
copper, brass.
51 x 38 x 7" (130 x 97 x 18 cm)

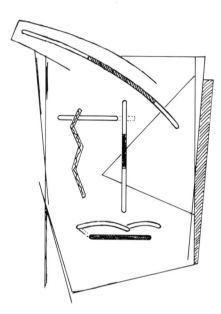

It was discovered at an early age that I was allergic to frankincense, the incense that wafts throughout the Serbian Orthodox religion; I would faint whenever I went to church. This was somewhat unfortunate as I did love the icons, the symbols, and the pageantry, even if I didn't love the male dominance and consequent subjugation of women. The Virgin Mary, Mother of God, did not play partial equalizer in this religion as she does for Catholics.

My family prided itself on the fact that my grandfather's marble quarries had supplied much of the marble for the churches in Jugoslavia and eastern Europe before the Communist takeover. I have toured the churches and monasteries along the backroads of Jugoslavia and have studied the Byzantine icons, frescoes and mosaics. They do glow and remain a powerful influence in my work.

In 1981, while waiting for a delayed plane in Tuscon, I drew the initial rough sketches for a body of work which I call "Icons."

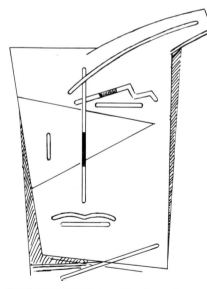

Initial sketches for these metal and neon icons were done at the Tuscon airport in 1981.

Following left hand page:
FALLING ANGEL
1983
Argon with mercury, helium and
krypton in glass tubing, aluminum,
copper, brass.
51 x 37 x 7" (130 x 94 x 18 cm)

Following right hand page:
HOLY GHOST
1983
Argon with mercury, helium and
krypton in glass tubing, aluminum,
copper, brass.
46½ x 36½ x 7" (118 x 93 x 18 cm)

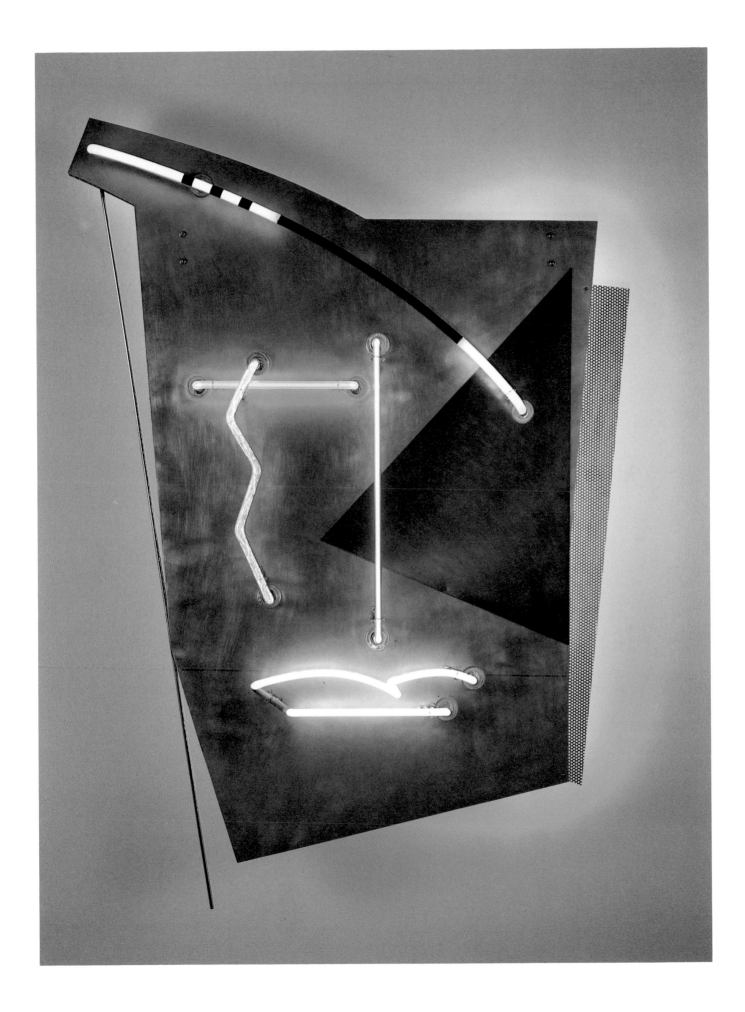

WOMAN WITH TATTOO
1980
Colored pencil on paper.
41 x 30" (104 x 76 cm)

Initial rough sketch for *The Warrior.*

Drawing is, for me, a very sensuous activity. The inspiration for a drawing is the very need to express love. Initial, tentative, exploratory marks, as in so much foreplay, give way to bolder strokes and massage-like motions as the image emerges. From slow, gentle caresses to quick, deliberate actions, the drawing assumes its own special feeling. There is pleasure in seeing what is beloved become revealed. And, finally, when the lips are worthy of being kissed, the drawing is done.

I have always loved to draw. And I kept right on drawing throughout painting class which I duly failed. I may have been the only art student in the history of Pratt Institute to fail painting. It was just too messy. (I never liked mudpies or fingerpainting as a child either.)

When I discovered that my drawings could actually become luminous, radiant, phosphorescent, it was as if I had discovered the secret of the universe.

African mask reference for *Witch Hunt.*

Preceding left hand page:
THE SORCERER (Portrait of
Nicholas von Sternberg, Jr.)
1985
Argon with mercury, neon and
helium in glass tubing, aluminum,
copper, brass.
51 x 41 x 7" (130 x 104 x 18 cm)

Preceding right hand page:
SAVING GRACE II
1984
Argon with mercury, neon and
helium in glass tubing, aluminum,
copper, brass.
60 x 48 x 10" (152 x 122 x 25 cm)

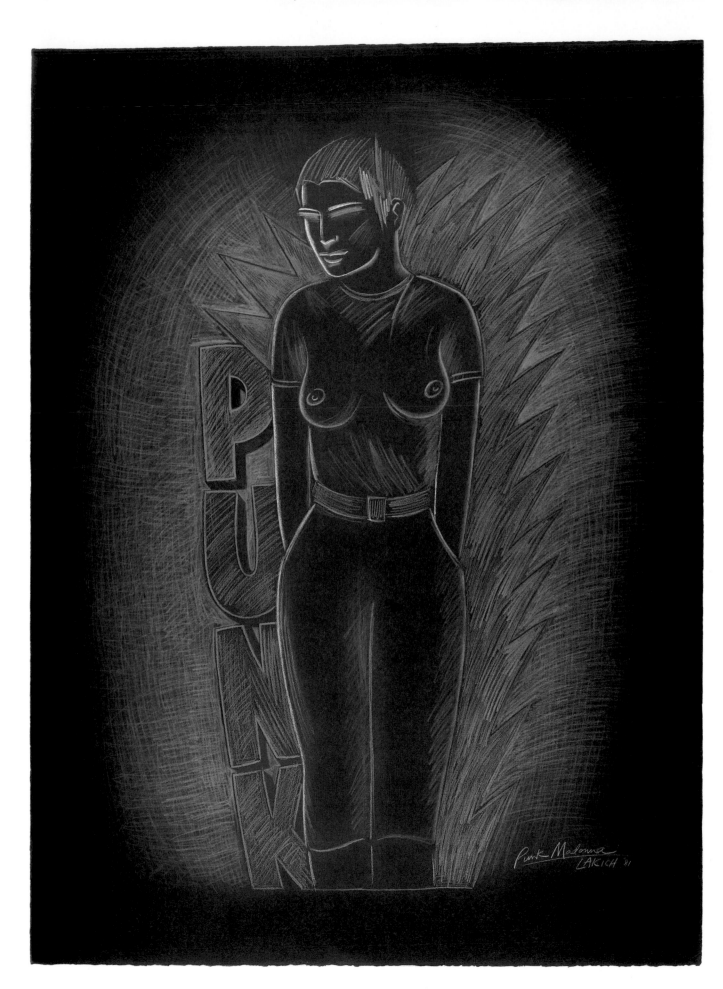

PUNK MADONNA, 1981. Colored pencil on paper. 41 x 30″ (104 x 76 cm).

SELF-PORTRAIT AS AN AMAZON RELAXING, 1981. Colored pencil on paper. 39½ x 30″ (99 x 76 cm).

SELF-PORTRAIT WITH CHAIN LINK FENCE, 1981. Colored pencil on paper. 26 x 22″ (66 x 56 cm).
Collection: Lt. Col. Ognjan I. Lakich, Sierra Vista, Arizona.

TATTOOED LOVER WITH BOXSPRING, 1985.   Colored pencil and pastels on paper.   42½ x 30″ (108 x 76 cm).

PORTRAIT OF JANE HANDEL, 1985. Colored pencil on paper. 44 x 30″ (112 x 76 cm).

SELF-PORTRAIT WITH NEON SCULPTURE, 1981. Colored pencil on paper. 41 x 25″ (104 x 64 cm).

DONNA IMPALED AS A
CONSTELLATION
1983
Argon, argon with mercury,
helium, krypton, and neon in glass
tubing, aluminum, copper, brass.
100 x 66 x 10″ (254 x 168 x 25 cm)

You are pale with longing
I am impaled for desire.

Artist and muse pose with celestial body, 1983.

I wanted to create a portrait of Donna Tracy that captured the essence of her spirit, a spirit that was deeply engaged in cosmology and the human form in relation to it. Donna posed for photographs and drawings, and I was able to create a beautiful monument to her, so that she may be included in the heavens among Aries, Sagittarius, Gemini, and all the rest.

With this sculpture I attempted for the first time to cut a detailed human figure out of metal. It surprised me that it was almost as sensual a process as drawing, although far more difficult. Sawing out a nose, a mouth, a shoulder, a hand was another way of bringing someone to life. But sawing, filing and sanding 1-inch honeycomb aluminum was extremely nerve-wracking. I had to stop frequently so that the vibration to my body would not become too severe. In the end, my hands and arms were numb for a week anyway.

One always hopes that the Pygmalion legend might indeed be true—that the sculpture would suddenly spring to life and fall madly in love with its creator.

Donna Impaled as a Constellation was first exhibited in the *At Home* exhibition, curated by Arlene Raven, at the Long Beach Museum of Art in 1983.

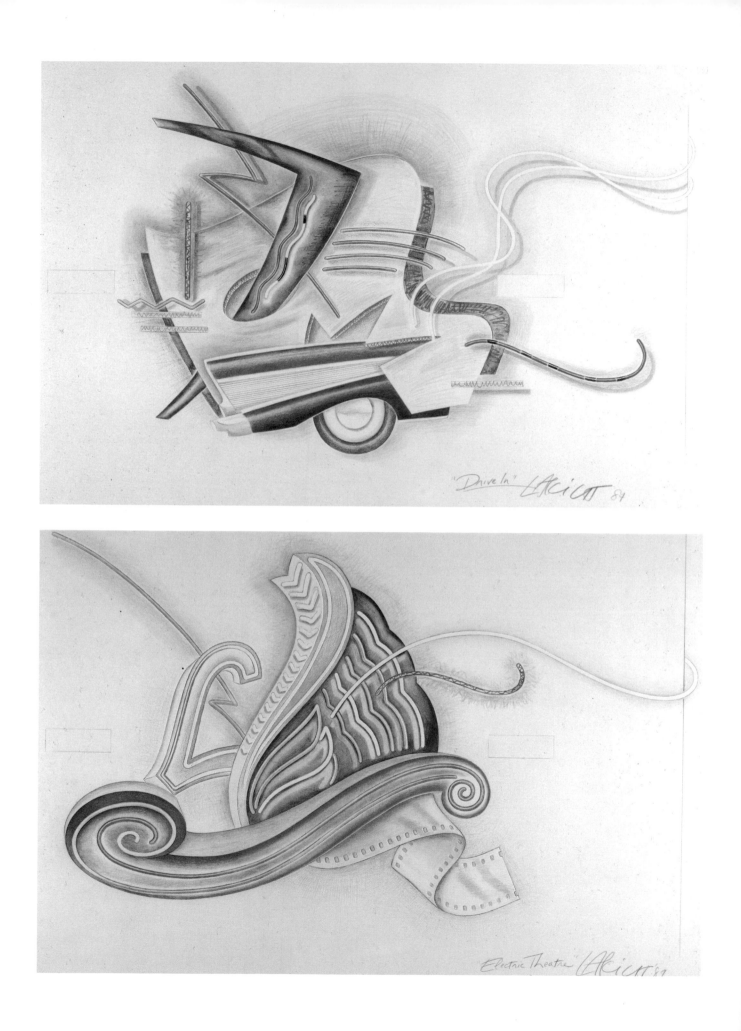

"Drive In" LACICT 87

"Electric Theatre" LACICT 87

DRIVE-IN
1984
Argon with mercury and neon in
glass tubing, aluminum, copper,
brass, '57 Chevy fender, tire.
216 x 120 x 24″ (549 x 305 x 61 cm)
Collection: Unity Savings,
Beverly Hills, California.

Built in 1931, Dolores Restaurant was one of the
original drive-in restaurants in Los Angeles. It was
torn down in 1981.

Opposite page:
DRIVE-IN (drawing)
1984
Colored pencil on paper.
26¼ x 37½ ″ (67 x 95 cm)
Collection: Unity Savings,
Beverly Hills, California.

ELECTRIC THEATER
1984
Colored pencil on paper.
26¼ x 38½ ″ (67 x 98 cm)
Collection: Unity Savings,
Beverly Hills, California.

Drive-In was commissioned by Unity Savings for their new Beverly Hills office. At the corner of Wilshire and La Cienega Boulevards (known as "Restaurant Row"), it is located on the former site of Dolores Restaurant, famous for being one of the original drive-in restaurants in Los Angeles. Dolores had been torn down against the will of its owner and long-term patrons and was replaced by a large office building. Unity Savings happened to be one of the tenants. Because a savings and loan relies on the support of local residents and businesses, I thought it would be exciting and appropriate to create a tribute to Dolores Restaurant.

For research, I set out to soak up the atmosphere of some of the remaining coffee shops which had been built in the 40's and 50's. I ate cheeseburgers, fried onion rings, and deep-dish cherry pie, and I found many of the forms used in the sculpture. It was at the Dolores Restaurant in West Los Angeles that I did the scribble below. The vinyl chair became the basic shape of the large aluminum background. It holds a 3-dimensional copper boomerang, one of the zoom shapes of the 50's. The original Dolores drive-in had copper counters and doors with portholes. Because it had been designed for cars to order window service, a car was essential. I chose the '57 Chevy for its quintessential beauty, its fairly 2-dimensional contour, and its symbolic relation to America of the 1950's— the Age of Automobile.

The neon tubes add direction, energy and luminosity. In addition to the huge plate-glass windows which admit large doses of the Southern California sun, the bank is brightly-lit; because the sculpture had to function primarily in daytime, only the brightest possible neon tubes were used. The neon crackle adds a perpetual spark. The ambient sounds include a collage of pop songs from the 50's to the 80's.

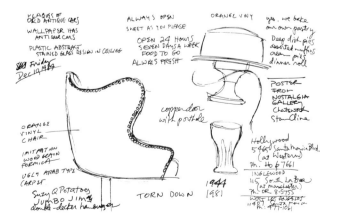

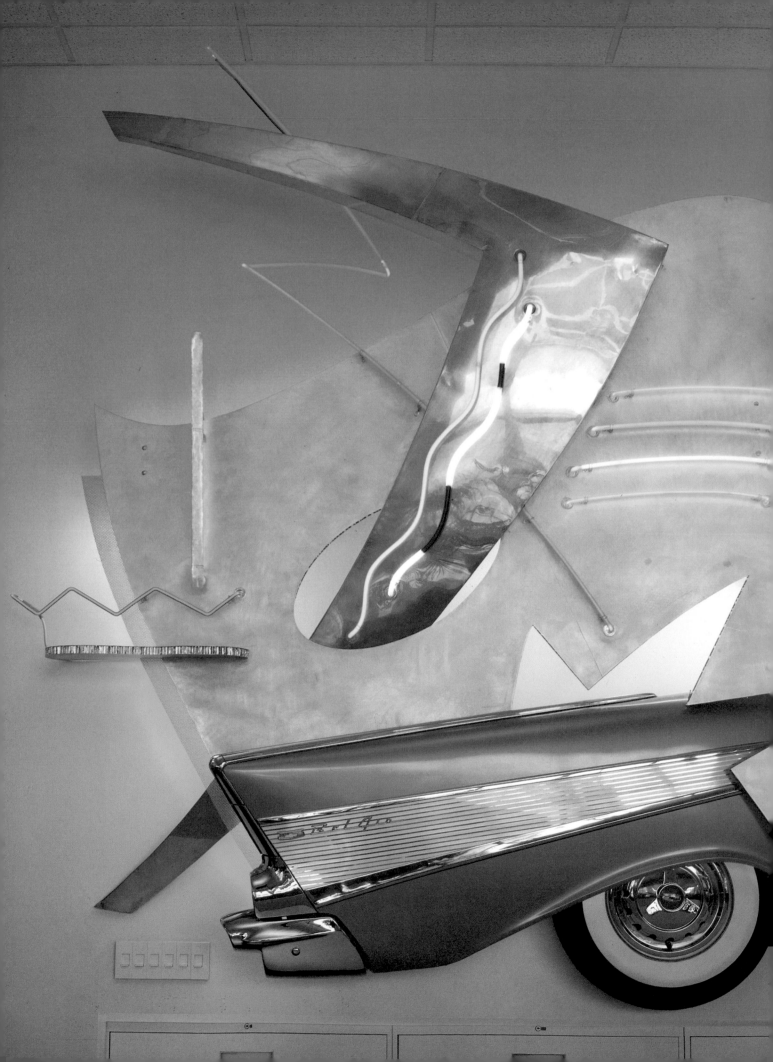

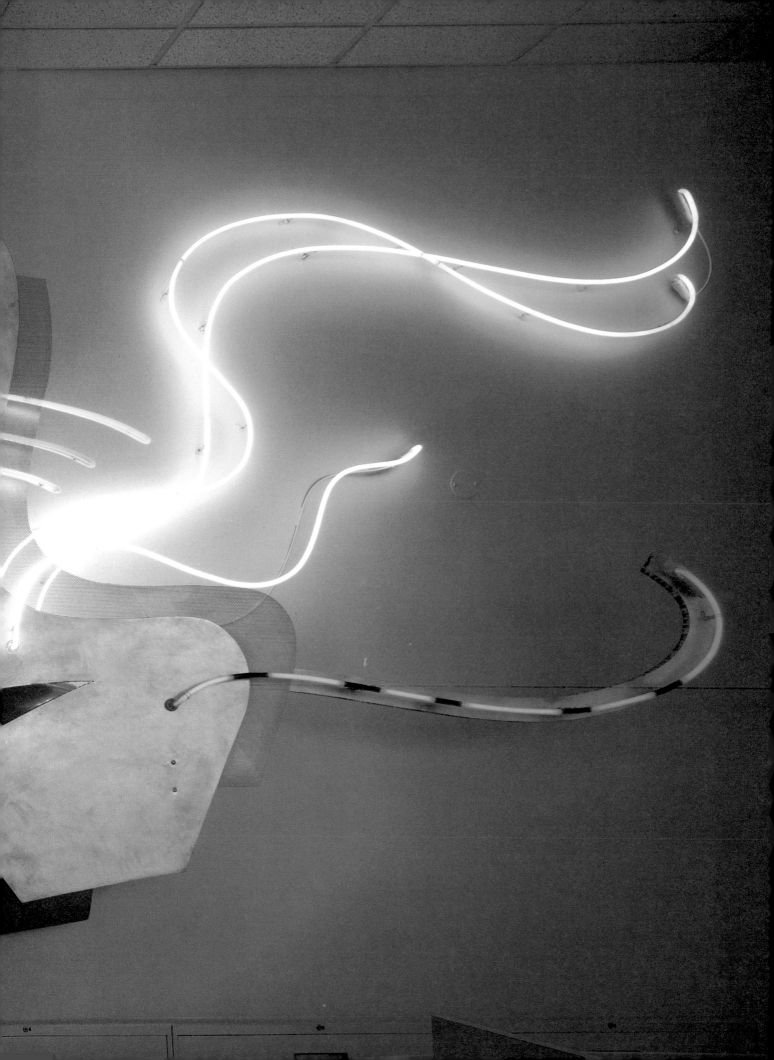

ELVIS
1985
Argon with mercury, neon and
helium in glass tubing, aluminum,
copper.
94 x 102 x 10″ (239 x 259 x 25 cm)

I was eleven years old when rock and roll began. I was living in Fort
Riley, Kansas, in 1955 when the Top 20 Hit Parade was broadcast over
radio on Saturday mornings for an hour. Then my family was transferred
to Germany, and the opportunity to hear rock and roll became even more
remote. But at some point during our four-year stay, Armed Forces Radio
held a contest for the best illustration of "The Purple Eater" which was a
hit song at the time. One of the soldiers in my father's company was a
talented cartoonist and, ever the art director even then, I mobilized my
father to have the soldier paint The Purple People Eater. For this I won a
bunch of Elvis Presley records. My admiration for his qualities as a singer
began then and has never waned. Elvis, most definitely, is the King of
Rock and Roll.

Artist's conception of "The Purple People Eater,"
circa 1958.

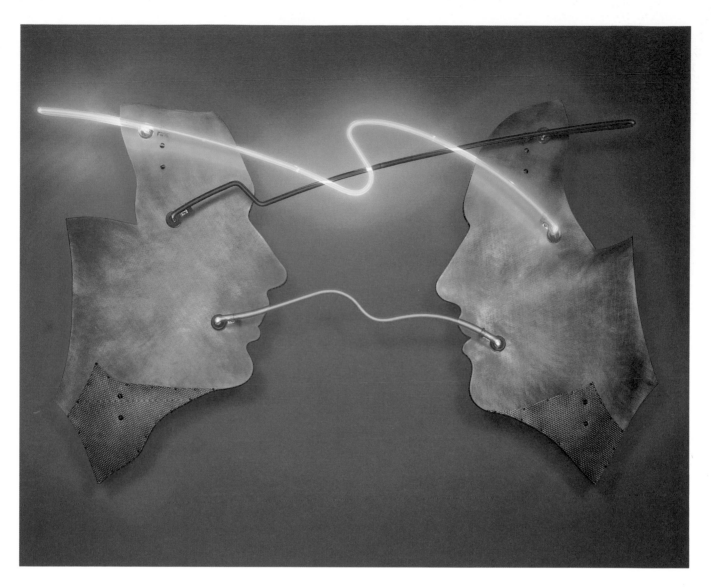

JONATHAN AND BILL
1985
Argon with mercury and neon in
glass tubing, aluminum, brass.
30 x 57 x 6″ (76 x 145 x 15 cm)
Collection: Jonathan Ahearn and
William Dry, Venice, California.

Opposite page:
THE GHOST OF JOHN COLTRANE
1985
Argon with mercury and neon in
glass tubing, aluminum, brass,
copper.
77 x 44 x 10″ (196 x 112 x 25 cm)
Collection: Jeff Atherton,
Los Angeles.

MONA
1981
Argon with mercury and neon in
glass tubing, photostat, masonite.
54½ x 39¼ x 7" (151 x 100 x 18 cm)
Collection: Museum of Neon Art.

*Your will realize your dreams by your
own efforts.*

Chinese fortune cookie

*The museum is a labor of love, a place
to show restored signs and innovative
art works.*

Michael Webb
Arts + Architecture

MONA sign being lifted onto the building in 1984.

Students from Richard Jenkins' UCLA extension
class working on the MONA sign.

In 1980 and 1981, I took stock of where my work was going and what it would mean in time. The neon sign industry had been dying for nearly 40 years, the beautiful colors of glass had gone out of production, new glass benders were not being trained (there were no schools). The medium was generally maligned, denigrated, and ultimately discarded. Perhaps bewildered by the technology, traditional museums and galleries rarely exhibited neon art. Exhibitions were rare and fleeting; I seldom got to see the work of other artists who used neon. In fact, I could count the neon artists I was even aware of on one hand.

I came to the conclusion that unless there was a permanent place, a museum, to exhibit, document and preserve this art form which I felt was synonymous with America itself, then my own work would be nowhere in 50 or 100 years. I realized that I was devoting my life to the creation of something that would be totally destroyed—never maintained, repaired or exhibited—unless I gave some energy toward creating that vehicle for its perpetuation.

With the help of Richard Jenkins I set about to do this in 1981 and found a lawyer, Peter Karlen, to draw up the nonprofit incorporation papers. We decided to call it the Museum of Neon Art, even though the museum is dedicated to all forms of electric and kinetic art. The acronym, MONA, with its reference to Leonardo's *Mona Lisa* was too good to pass up. By adding neon tubes to the single most important image in the history of art, we declared neon to be a fine art at last.

MONA, the only museum of its kind in the world, opened to the public in May of 1982. By changing exhibitions, usually every three months, artists, previously isolated, have been motivated to create new work. A spirit of inspiration and support has developed, resulting in tremendous growth for everyone involved, including myself. The classes we have taught have encouraged new people wanting to work in the medium. Neon has been revitalized. The media now frequently refers to the "renaissance" of neon. And I think our lady of light, the neon MONA, had something to do with it.

MUSEUM OF NEON ART

Installation views of my twenty-year retrospective exhibition, *Neon Lovers Glow in the Dark,* at the Museum of Neon Art, November 6, 1985 through April 26, 1986.

VAL'S CAFE
1974
Argon with mercury in glass
tubing, painted shaped metal case.
58 x 97 x 7" (147 x 246 x 18 cm)

HOT LUNCH
1979
Argon with mercury and neon in
glass tubing, painted metal.
41 x 49 x 8" (104 x 124 x 20 cm)
Commissioned by Seiniger
Advertising for the movie "Fame."
(The original title was "Hot Lunch.")

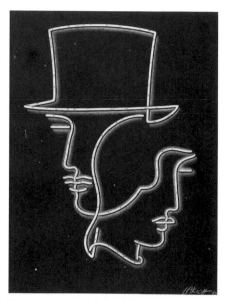

Neon drawing commissioned by Vanity Fair in
1981, never published.

Jim Dahlia bending one of the neon leaves for the
Loews Anatole Hotel.

*Neon is associated with the highest
aspirations and fantasies of the
American dream as well as the
lowest expression of commercialism
and banality. There is no other art
form that is as symbolic of the
American spirit.*

When I was in art school, there was a teacher who used to say, "If you want to do a drawing, skip a meal and buy an expensive piece of paper." I soon realized that given the cost of neon and the materials I wanted to use, I would quickly starve to death if I didn't figure out how to do a job that paid well. So I got into advertising and eventually became an art director specializing in motion picture and entertainment campaigns. Over the years I have had the opportunity to create neon designs for movies, posters, record covers, book covers, stage sets, magazine illustrations, stores and boutiques, computer software, environmental decor, awards programs, and as numerous gifts for Christmas, weddings and birthdays, including one for Los Angeles Mayor Tom Bradley and even a neon portrait of Rams owner Georgia Frontieri given to her by the team.

One of the most exciting commissions was for a mural of animating flamingos and floral designs. The 276 square foot installation is suspended over the dance floor of a restaurant/disco in the Loews Anatole Hotel in Dallas.

As people rediscover the incredible beauty, color, light and ambience that neon brings to an environment, innovations in the medium are expanding the range of its uses. Sadly, some cities have passed ordinances against neon and have called for the removal of existing neon signs. It is frightening to me that lawmakers can legislate against an entire art form— perhaps the only art form that has truly become symbolic of the American spirit.

C O M M E R C I A L   N E O N   W O R K

VENUS
1983
Argon with mercury, neon and
helium in glass tubing, photostat,
masonite, plexiglas.
34 x 48 x 8″ (86 x 122 x 20 cm)
Collection: Helga and Robert
Trachinger, Los Angeles.
On the cover of *The Magic of Neon*.

Opposite page:
DAZZLE DRAW
1984
Argon with mercury and neon in
glass tubing, photostat, masonite.
54 x 53 x 7″ (137 x 135 x 18 cm)
Commissioned by Chapman/
Sabatella Advertising and
Broderbund Software, Inc. for the
box of an Apple IIc/IIe program.

Sketch for a neon image to symbolize the
At Home exhibition at the Long Beach
Museum of Art in 1983.

This trailer art for the MGM/Blake Edwards film "Victor/Victoria" was originally to be a large animated neon display. It ended up being rendered through film animation techniques and intercut with live action musical sequences from the movie. Commissioned by Intralink, 1982.

Four of the eight drawings for an animated neon mural designed to hang in an octagonal truss over the dance floor of Mistral, a restaurant/disco in the Loews Anatole Hotel in Dallas, Texas, 1985.

New York skyline for Manhattan, Inc. magazine, 1984.

Cover design based on the Nuart marquee.

Neon logo for Fox's 1975 campaign.

Sign for a studio/boutique in Hollywood, 1982.

Sign for a Beverly Hills shop for urban cowboy clothing, 1980.

Record album cover for Columbia Records, 1979.

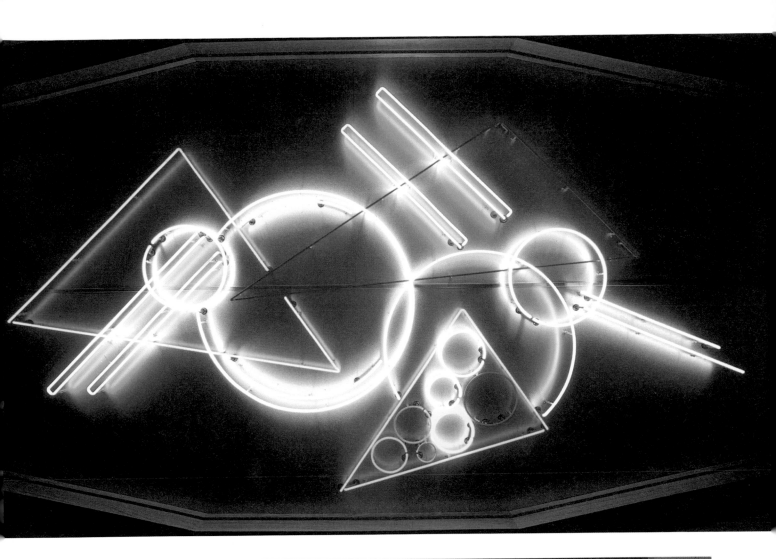

I created this neon ceiling for a Kentucky Fried Chicken restaurant on Olympic Boulevard in Los Angeles, 1985.

BIOGRAPHY

My father began his military career as a second lieutenant in the King's Royal Guards in Jugoslavia just prior to World War II.

My mother, brother, and I in Monterey, California during the time my father was in Korea.

Stonehenge in 1964 before graffitti and barbed wire ruined it.

1944 — Born in Washington, D.C. on June 4th.

Captured by the Germans when they overran Jugoslavia, my father escaped and emigrated in 1941 to the United States where he was drafted into the American Army. In Washington, D.C., he met and married my mother who worked at the Jugoslav Embassy. Flying with a freedom force of ex-patriot Jugoslav airmen, he was shot down over Bulgaria and spent the first year of my life in a prison camp.

1951-53 — Father sent to the Korean War. Family relocated to Monterrey, California.

1953-55 — Assigned to Fort Riley, Kansas.

All I remember is that rock and roll began, and everyone wore pink and gray or pink and black (except the military who always wore olive green and khaki).

1955-59 — Transferred to Frankfurt, Germany.

I attended the American school for children of the Armed Forces and went to summer camp in Switzerland and Denmark. We travelled throughout Europe and as far as Istanbul.

1959-60 — Returned to the U.S. and Baltimore, Maryland.

The first day of class at Dundalk High, Mr. Laubheimer asked his 10th grade art class, "How many of you like art?" When only a few timid hands went up, mine included, he sent the rest of the students to the music department. He was a great art teacher.

1960-62 — Junior and senior year at Arundel High School, halfway between Baltimore and Washington, D.C.

I designed the yearbook and took classes at The Maryland Art Institute.

1962-64 — College at Pratt Institute in Brooklyn, New York.

Pratt Institute was a converted shoe factory and the campus was small. Within the art school competition was fierce; I worked all night several times a week in order to complete assignments in 2-dimensional design, 3-dimensional design or color classes. In the little time left I took the subway to Greenwich Village and heard Bob Dylan, Joan Baez, Dave van Ronk and others. Summers were spent with my family who was stationed once again in Germany. With friends I drove to England and saw Stonehenge before graffitti and barbed wire enveloped it. Stonehenge is the most magnificent and mysterious monument I have ever seen and ranks with Death Valley as one of the wonders of the world.

At Pratt I started learning printmaking—silkscreen, etching, lithography and photography. I considered becoming a fashion photographer but decided photography was too easy. You can't point a canvas or a blank piece of paper at a subject and have something emerge like you can with a camera. Still, I was becoming bored with art school and spent a lot of time seeing double bills of foreign films. Thinking that perhaps filmmaking might be what I wanted to do with my life, I took a leave of absence from Pratt in order to go to film school.

1964-65 — Moved to London.

The London School of Film Technique offered a thorough technical training course with months of lengthy lectures before I ever got to handle a camera. After a couple of unfinished 16mm projects, I managed to complete an 8-minute 35mm film titled "The Long Anticipated Journey of the Mouth of the Mona Lisa." It combined live action with animation, and it is curious that twenty years later I would still be involved with Mona's smile. Having learned that filmmaking is too dependent on an entire group's talents or lack of them, I came to appreciate the solitary nature of art.

1965-67 — Returned to New York and Pratt Institute.

This time I really tried to figure out what aspect of art interested me. I had always loved looking at neon signs, and when I saw an exhibition of neon and plastic work by Martial Raysée I was hooked on the unexplored possibilities of neon as art rather than just as signs. My first experiments incorporated tiny light bulbs; when I plugged in my first completed sculpture, all the light bulbs exploded. Thus I learned the difference between parallel and series wiring. Sometime after that I built a tribute to my grandmother using plexiglas, vacuum formed letters which spelled out her name, a horse skull I had found in Jugoslavia, and a light blue neon swiggle that I had a neon shop make for me. Onto the back of the translucent white plexi, I projected a film I had made of her. My teachers at Pratt were dumbfounded. They asked me if I wanted to switch from the fine arts department into advertising. I graduated from Pratt Institute with a Bachelor of Fine Arts degree, and I never went back.

1967-68 — Worked as a caseworker for the New York Department of Social Services.

One day on my way home from work, I was attacked on the subway by a gang of teenage girls with over a hundred people just watching. I decided that New York wasn't for me.

1968	Moved to San Francisco. This was the prettiest city I'd seen next to Paris, but after a couple of months I felt oppressed by its infatuation with all things Victorian. I was into plastic and lights.
1968-70	Moved to Los Angeles. I had never had an idea for any of my work in San Francisco, so when I moved to L.A. and got some ideas, I knew I was in the right place. My first job was at *CYCLE NEWS* in Long Beach.
1972	Exhibitions at the La Jolla Museum of Art, La Jolla, California, at Womanspace and at 707 Gallery in Los Angeles. On the evening of the 707 opening the heavens put forth the most gorgeous sunset anybody had ever seen, as if to prove that artists should always remember their place.
1973	Exhibitions at the Los Angeles County Museum of Art, *Neon Signs & Symbols* at California State College in Fullerton curated by Dextra Frankel, at Orlando Gallery in Encino, California and at Womanspace.
1974	First solo exhibition, *Scar,* at Womanspace in its new location in The Woman's Building in Los Angeles.
1974-78	First studio at 4912 Fountain Avenue in Hollywood.
1974-81	Employed by Seiniger Advertising in Los Angeles. The company specialized in motion picture advertising; I designed movie posters, brochures and trailers.
1975	Exhibitions at Gilbert Galleries in San Francisco and at Pasadena City College in Pasadena, California
1976	Inaugural solo show at L.A. Louver Gallery in Venice, California.
1977	Solo show, *Draw Me Nearer,* at my studio sponsored by L.A. Louver Gallery.
1978	Exhibitions at Anhalt/Barnes Gallery, Los Angeles and *A Shade of Light* at The Fine Art Museum of San Francisco. Solo show at Galerie au Fond de la Cour on Rue du Dragon, Paris. I built the sculptures in Paris during the three months preceding the opening. The gallery director was Gabrielle Maubrie.
1979-81	*No Vacancy* travelled through The Netherlands and Germany in *Feministiche Kunst International,* originating at Haags Gemmentemuseum, Haag, Netherlands.
1980	Bought the building at 704 Traction Avenue in downtown Los Angeles for my studio. Exhibited in *The Great American Lesbian Art Show* at the Woman's Building and at the Downey Museum of Art in Downey, California. Met Chryssa who is considered to be the first artist to use neon in a fine art context. I had to go to New York to art direct a photo session for the movie "Eyewitness" with Sigourney Weaver. A major disagreement between photographer and star over the styling of the photo left me with a lot of free time while they fought it out. I tried to get in touch with Chryssa whom I had always wanted to meet, but no one I talked to knew where she was or how to contact her. Then on one of my last days in New York I was walking back to my hotel from the Guggenheim Museum, and I stopped in a delicatessen on Madison Avenue, and there was Chryssa. I said, "Are you Chryssa?" And she said, "Of course, how did you know?" Chryssa told me that in 1965 she had six pages in *LIFE* magazine but still couldn't pay her rent.
1981	Founded the Museum of Neon Art in Los Angeles with Richard Jenkins. Started Calko and Lakich Advertising.
1982	Exhibited in *Extended Sensibilities: Homosexual Presence in Contemporary Art* curated by Daniel J. Cameron at The New Museum in New York.
1982-85	Exhibited in various shows at the Museum of Neon Art, and taught neon design there. Taught drawing at The Otis Art Institute of Parsons School of Design, Los Angeles.
1983	Created new work for a room in The Long Beach Museum of Art as part of the *At Home* exhibition curated by Arlene Raven. Curated *Ladies of the Night,* an exhibition of neon images of women at the Museum of Neon Art.
1984	The Museum of Neon Art sent an exhibition of neon sculpture by ten artists including myself to the Seibu Museum of Art in Tokyo, Japan. I travelled to Tokyo to supervise the installation and returned via Hong Kong and Hawaii. The exhibition was voted one of the years ten best exhibitions in Japan, in the company of Rembrandt, Salvador Dali, and Laurie Anderson.
1985-86	Twenty-year retrospective exhibition, *Neon Lovers Glow in the Dark,* curated by Richard Jenkins and Gayle Rendleman at the Museum of Neon Art.

One of many similar graffitti slogans during the sixties.

Banjo and I had similar personalities —with barks worse than our bite.

Mary Carter, Gayle Rendleman, myself and Richard Jenkins after finishing the installation.

BIBLIOGRAPHY

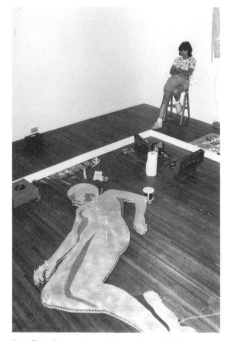

Installing *Donna Impaled as a Constellation* at
The Long Beach Museum of Art in 1983.

Deciding on the placement of a sculpture during
the installation of my retrospective at the Museum
of Neon Art in 1985.

Ainslee, Peter. "Let There Be NEON!," *TWA Ambassador,* vol. 18, no. 9, September 1985, pp. 81-86.

"Art and Artisan Lili Lakich," *Designers West,* vol. 25, no. 12, October 1978, pp. 72-75.

Askey, Ruth. "Lili Lakich's Neon Portraits," *Artweek,* November 5, 1977, p.5.

"Available Light," Kristin Zethren, ed., *Eye 8,* 1983, p. 9.

Bermann-Enn, Beate. "Lili Lakich," *ArtScene,* vol. 5, no. 4, December 1985, pp. 9-10.

Brown, Nancy. "Financial Institutions' New Values, New Images," *Designers West,* vol. 32, no. 4, February 1985, cover and pp. 70-83.

Crane, Tricia. "Neon as Art—It's a Bright Idea," *The Daily News,* September 25, 1981, cover and pp. 3, 7, 29.

Diedrichs, Gary. "Jewels of the Night," *Datsun Discovery,* vol. 4, no. 2, Summer 1980, p.4.

Donahue, Marlena. "Neon Art Museum Exhibit; It's a Gas," *Los Angeles Times,* December 29, 1984, "Calendar," pp. 1, 3.

Drew, Nancy. "Neon Art Comes Out of the Dark," *Reader,* vol. 7, no. 14, January 25, 1985, pp. 1, 8-9, 18.

Gable, Mona. "Electric Art: The Neon Renaissance," *Savvy,* vol. 6, no. 8, August 1985, pp. 60-61.

————. "The Neon Renaissance: Recharging an Electric Art," *The Wall Street Journal,* May 9, 1985, p. 30.

Gamwell, Lynn. "Approaches to Neon," *Artweek,* vol. 9, no. 10, March 11, 1978.

Gersten, Ross. "MONA: Lighting Up the Arts with Neon," *Civic Center News/Downtown News,* August 31, 1982, p.4.

Grand, Jeannie. "Neon Knights," *The Daily Breeze,* January 29, 1984, "People," pp. E1-E2.

Hyman, Jackie. "Unique Art Museum Puts Neon in a Favorable Light," The Associated Press; *Salinas Californian,* August 21, 1985, p. 15.

Kirsch, Jonathan. "Alternating Currents," *New West,* vol. 2, no. 21, October 10, 1977, pp. 50-51.

Lakich, Lili. "What's New in Neon," *Los Angeles Times Magazine,* vol. 2, no. 3, January 19, 1986, cover and p. 15.

"Lili Lakich," *Artweek,* February 23, 1974, p. 6.

Menzies, Neal. "Sexual Identity and Anonymity," *Artweek,* vol. 11, no. 20, May 24, 1980, p. 4.

"MONA: Museum of Neon Art," *Signs of the Times,* vol. 203, no. 123, December 1981, pp. 81-83, 109.

Moufarrege, Nicolas A. "Lavender: On Homosexuality and Art," *Arts Magazine,* October 1982, vol. 57, no. 2, pp. 78-87.

Muchnic, Suzanne. "Exhibition of Lesbian Artworks," *Los Angeles Times,* May 27, 1980, "Calendar," p. 1.

Nachman, Steve. " Gallery Guest: Lakich, High on Neon," *Paris Metro,* vol. 3, no. 22, October 25, 1978, p. 31.

"Neon," *The Daily Report,* April 19, 1985, "Weekend," p. 41.

Ohland, Gloria. "Lili Lakich's Neon Disneyland," *L.A. Weekly,* vol. 5, no. 42, September 16, 1983, p.4.

Plagens, Peter. "Reviews: Los Angeles," *Artforum,* September 1974, pp. 88-89.

"Print's Regional Design Annual '84," *Print,* vol. 36, no. 4, July/August 1984, p.68.

Raven, Arlene. "Your Goodbye Left Me with Eyes That Cry," *Chrysalis,* no. 5 (1978), pp. 53-56.

————. and Ruth Iskin. "Through the Peephole: Toward a Lesbian Sensibility in Art," *Chrysalis,* vol. 3, October 1977, pp. 19-31.

Reed, J.D. "The Canvas Is the Night," *Time,* vol. 125, no. 23, June 10, 1985, pp. 70-71.

Rico, Diana. "Artistic Signs of the Times," *L.A. Life, Daily News,* December 4, 1985, p. 13.

Takahama, Valerie. "Neon Glows for New Admirers," *Press Telegram,* September 8, 1985, pp. J3-J4.

von Eckhardt, Wolf. "User-Friendly Winners," *Time,* vol. 125, no. 1, January 7, 1985, pp. 104-105.

Webb, Michael. "Lights of the Night," *Sky Magazine,* vol. 13, no. 2, February 1984, pp. 114-118.

————. "Neon Then and Now," *Art and Architecture,* vol. 1, no. 3 (1983), pp. 61-63.

Wilson, William. "Artwalk," *Los Angeles Times,* September 29, 1972.

_____. "Symbols and Signs in Neon," *Los Angeles Times,* March 9, 1973.

_____. "A Paean to Neon," *Los Angeles Times Magazine,* vol. 2, no. 3, January 19, 1986, pp. 12-14.

Uyeda, Seiko. "Art Forum '86." *Kateigaho,* April 1986, pp. 216-218.

Yorkin, Nicole. "Liquid Light: Neon Makes a Dazzling Debut at L.A.'s New Museum of Neon Art," *Los Angeles Herald Examiner,* May 9, 1982, "California Living," pp. 14-17.

Zone, Ray. "Spectral Psalms." *Artweek,* vol. 17, no. 9, March 8, 1986, p.6.

BOOKS AND CATALOGS

Booth-Clibborn, Edward (ed.). *American Illustration 1982/83.* New York: American Illustration, Inc., 1982.

_____. *European Illustration 1982.* London: European Illustration, 1981.

Cameron, Daniel J. "The Beautiful Lover," *Extended Sensibilities: Homosexual Presence in Contemporary Art.* New York: The New Museum, 1982.

Halbertsma, Marlite (ed.). *Feministische Kunst Internationaal.* The Hague, Netherlands: Haags Gemeentemuseum, 1978.

Neon Art from the West Coast. Tokyo: The Seibu Museum of Art, 1984.

Raven, Arlene. *At Home.* Long Beach: Long Beach Museum of Art, 1983.

Webb, Michael. *The Magic of Neon.* Salt Lake City: Gibbs M. Smith, Inc., Peregrine Smith Books, 1983.

Wilson, William. *Neon Signs and Symbols.* Fullerton, California: Art Gallery, California State University, 1973.

FILMS AND VIDEO

Buttignol, Rudy and Ken Ketter, dir. *Neon, An Electric Memoir.* Rudy, Inc., 1984. 26 minutes.

Ladies of the Night. Writ. Anne Marie Piersimoni. Falcon Cable, October 1983.

Mary's Go Round. Writ. Mary Wallace. NBC-TV, October 16, 1983.

Mundo Latino. SIN-TV, November 1, 1983.

Neon-Light-Art. Prod. Peter Reichelt. German Television ZDF, July-August 1985. 30 minutes.

Neon Magic. "Two on the Town," CBS-TV, October 13, 1982.

News at Six and Eleven. KCBS-TV, June 18, 1984.

Ripley's Believe It or Not. ABC-TV, November 6, 1983.

Ruth, Sheila and Jan Zimmerman, dir. and prod. *Signed by a Woman.* 1978. 60 minutes.

Schmidt, Richard, dir. *Friday at Sunset.* With Howard Stevens. KCBS-TV, January 17, 1986.

Today Show. Prod. Julie Ladner. Channel 9 Australia, January 1986.

Videolog. Prod. Karen Minsberg. KCET-TV, November 1984. Repeated throughout 1985.

AWARDS

1978   The Gay Academic Union: Fine Arts Award

1981   20th Annual Society of Illustrators Los Angeles: Winner, Corporate Category

1984   The Women's Building: VESTA Award for Visual Art
       American Association of Museums: Award of Distinction
       City of Los Angeles: Mayor's Certificate of Appreciation
       Time Magazine: Poster of the Year.

1986   Listed in the Fifteenth (1986-1987) Edition of *Who's Who of American Women*

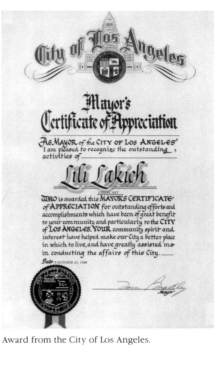

Award from the City of Los Angeles.

Los Angeles Times Magazine cover, 1986.

PHOTO CREDITS

Lili Lakich and Richard Jenkins in front of *Blessed Oblivion* for *THE DAILY NEWS* story on the opening of the Museum of Neon Art in 1981.